Stadium Stories™ Series

W9-CFC-348

Stadium Stories:

USC Trojans

Jim Gigliotti

INSIDERS' GUIDE®

GUILFORD, CONNECTICUT
AN IMPRINT OF THE GLOBE PEQUOT PRESS

INSIDERS' GUIDE®

Text design: Casey Shain
Cover photos: *front cover:* Matt Leinart (Nam Y. Huh/AP); *back cover:* top, John McKay (AP); bottom, Rodney Peete (Mark Terrill/AP)

Library of Congress Cataloging-in-Publication Data
Gigliotti, Jim.
    Stadium stories : USC Trojans / Jim Gigliotti. – 1st ed.
      p. cm. – (Stadium stories series)
    ISBN 0-7627-3779-4
    1. University of Southern California—Football—History. 2. Southern California Trojans (Football team)—History. I. Title: USC Trojans. II. Title. III. Series.

GV958.U565G54 2005
796.332'63'0979494 – dc22
                                       2005046120

Manufactured in the United States of America
First Edition/First Printing

To Wendy, Dante, and Sophia—my family outside the Trojan Family—and to the late Robert A. Jeffrey, Jr., M.D., who originally set me on the road to USC and for whose help in so many ways I will always be grateful.

Acknowledgments

Over the past quarter century, I've had the great pleasure to talk with many Trojan alumni about their football-playing days at the school. I would like to thank them all, but especially Damon Bame, Clarence Davis, Craig Fertig, Marv Goux, Pat Haden, John McKay (the coach's son), Anthony Muñoz, Toby Page, Nick Pappas, Mike Rae, Tim Rossovich, Paul Salata, Rod Sherman, and Richard Wood—their recollections in particular helped shape this book.

I'd also like to thank author Jim Perry, a wonderful mentor and friend whose previous collaboration with John McKay on the coach's autobiography was a valuable reference source. So, too, were previous works on USC's football history by Mal Florence, Joe Jares, and Ken Rappoport, as well as Rose Bowl history by Rick Hamlin. Former senior manager and athletic-department employee Dave Rush, who is now a commercial real estate executive, helped immensely with recalling names and events over the past several decades.

Thanks, also, to Jim Buckley of Shoreline Publishing Group in Santa Barbara, California, who got the ball rolling on this project, and to editors Mary Norris at The Globe Pequot Press and Mike Urban of Urban Publishing Services.

And finally I owe a special debt of gratitude to USC sports information director Tim Tessalone. He not only patiently answered various queries relative to this book, but—as my first boss in the "real world" in the 1980s—also taught me more than he will ever know.

Contents

The Trojan Family

Not long after I'd arrived at USC as an eighteen-year-old freshman in the fall of 1980, I was assigned to do a story on the history of Trojan ice hockey for an athletic department publication. Despite my initial skepticism that they actually played ice hockey in sunny Southern California, I phoned Arnold Eddy, a former player, coach, and graduate manager (roughly the equivalent of today's athletic director) who later headed the USC Alumni Association.

Mr. Eddy assured me that hockey really had been an intercollegiate sport at USC (it's still played there as a club sport) and that it had been very successful in the 1930s and 1940s, even claiming a national championship in 1941. A short time later I was in Mr. Eddy's living room, sipping coffee, perusing old newspaper clippings, and turning the worn pages of past *El Rodeo* college yearbooks.

It's not just that Mr. Eddy was a very nice man (he was) or took pity on strangers (or more accurately, on bumbling teenagers working on their first internships). It was as if I was a member of the family. And I was: It was my first indoctrination to the concept of the Trojan Family.

Sound corny? Sure it's corny. But every USC student, past or present, has heard the expression, "You're a Bruin (or Cougar or Bear or Wildcat or whatever) for four years; you're a Trojan for life." And everywhere you go in Southern California, doctors, lawyers, financial professionals, people in the entertainment industry—and longtime university employees such as Mr. Eddy—consider themselves Trojans first and foremost.

Family members help out other family members. So Mr. Eddy welcomed me into his living room and gave me more information than I could ever use. That living room, by the way, was just a stone's throw from the venerable Shrine Auditorium across the street from the USC campus.

The Shrine Auditorium is perhaps best known as the site of the motion picture industry's annual Academy Awards for many years in the 1980s and 1990s (and as recently as 2001). It has hosted many other awards shows and events, too. But back in the 1940s, the Shrine also was the place that USC hosted UCLA in a basketball game. That's right. The stage was transformed into a makeshift basketball court with a hoop at each end. (Such an archaic setting still may be preferable to the decrepit Sports Arena, which at last will give way to USC's new home basketball arena in 2006—ironically, about a quarter mile from the Shrine.)

The saga of the Shrine is just a small slice of USC's storied history. The university was founded in 1880 and boasts today that it is the "oldest and largest private research university in the western half of the United States."

The school was selected in 2000 as the college of the year by the *Time/Princeton Review College Guide*. Its faculty is among the most respected in the nation. Distinguished alumni include the likes of Herb Alpert, Neil Armstrong, Art Buchwald, Warren Christopher, Frank Gehry, Marilyn Horne, General Norman Schwarzkopf, and scores of motion picture actors, actresses, producers, and directors.

And yet there's also no denying that the university is known worldwide—fair or not—in large part because of its football team. Through 2004 the Trojans had won eleven national championships, fielded 135 All-Americans, and produced six Heisman Trophy winners. More USC players have been selected in the first round of the annual NFL draft than those of any other school, and hundreds of players from USC have gone on to play pro football.

In addition to the laundry list of high-profile awards and accomplishments on the field, USC football is also the marching band and the song girls, the tunes "Conquest" and "Fight On,"

Traveler, and the Coliseum. It is the locker room tunnel, Tommy Trojan, the Rose Bowl on New Year's Day, and not just one, but two annual rivalry games. And that's not just stuff for the alumni and fans, either. Players and coaches feel it, too.

In 1993 former head coach John Robinson (1976 to 1982) returned to the Trojan sidelines after a decade away, most of it spent in professional football with the NFL's Los Angeles Rams. "I missed the horse," he said. Robinson, who was known for his sense of humor, wasn't trying to be funny. "I can't wait to see the horse and hear 'Conquest' again," he said.

"The horse definitely got the adrenaline going when I was playing," said defensive back Nate Shaw, who served as a co-captain on USC's 1966 team and later as an assistant coach at the school.

The horse not only inspires Trojan players, it also gets under the skin of their opponents. Years after watching the Trojans run roughshod over his Fighting Irish in meetings at the Coliseum in 1972 and 1974, thus drawing Traveler out of the tunnel time and again, Notre Dame coach Ara Parseghian complained of having nightmares about the white horse. (We think he was joking.)

Washington State head coach Mike Price once tried to fire up his underdog team at practice the week before the school played a game against USC in the 1990s. A costumed Trojan sitting atop an imitation Traveler pranced into the Cougars practice. Price pretended to be surprised—then pulled a prop gun out of his pocket and shot the horse with blanks.

The Trojans (not to mention animal activists) didn't find that so funny. USC got the last laugh by beating the Cougars the first eight times the schools met during Price's tenure.

"Fight On"

USC's famous fight song was written in 1922 by Milo Sweet, a dental student at the school, and Glen Grant. Here are the words to "Fight On":

Fight On for ol' SC
Our men Fight On to victory.
Our alma mater dear,
Looks up to you
Fight On and win
For ol' SC
Fight On to victory
Fight On!

Linebacker Lofa Tatupu flashes the "Victory" sign. Joe Robbins

The drum major is part of the pageantry of USC football. Joe Robbins

Traveler was the brainchild in the early 1960s of Bob Jani, the school's director of special events, and Eddie Tannenbaum, an undergraduate at the university. After watching rider Richard Saukko atop his white horse in the 1961 Rose Parade, they convinced Saukko to come out to USC games astride his mount and in costume. Ever since, the horse makes an appearance whenever the Trojans score.

Saukko rode the horse himself through the end of the 1988 season, and a series of riders have succeeded him. There also have been several Travelers. The horses have been various breeds, but they are always pure white.

I often used to stand near Traveler at the mouth of the Coliseum tunnel while waiting for the Trojans to take the field in pregame. It is a powerful and majestic animal, and when the horse breaks into a full gallop in front of the USC student section before a game, it is a marvelous sight.

Traveler wasn't the first horse to appear at Trojan games as a mascot, though. Rockazar patrolled the sidelines in the mid- to late 1950s, and as many as three decades before that, another white horse appeared at USC games for a period of several seasons.

Long before Traveler made his debut in the Coliseum in 1961, USC also had a dog—named George Tirebiter—as an unofficial mascot. Tirebiter earned his name by chasing cars along University Avenue on the school's campus, a stretch long since closed to through traffic. The mutt was adopted by the football program and spent a decade as its mascot from 1940 to 1950.

Eventually there were several incarnations of George Tirebiter through 1957. The original Tirebiter died in 1950, when—you guessed it—he was run over by a car.

Another dog was the unofficial, in-house mascot of USC's powerful 1972 team. That year, hulking All-America tackle Pete Adams took in a small, stray mutt that he affectionately named Turd. The canine would follow his adoptive father into the huddle during practice, and after practice he'd run wind sprints with the team.

You might think that a little dog running around the practice field would annoy a no-nonsense coach such as John McKay. To the contrary, McKay said, "I really liked that dog." Like him or not, the dog did not accompany the Trojans each Saturday to the Coliseum.

USC has played its home games at the Los Angeles Memorial Coliseum since 1923. Its first varsity game there was a 23–7 rout of Pomona on October 6 of that year. Through the end of the 2004 season, Troy had won 380 games at the site, while losing only 122 and tying 27. That's a winning percentage of .744, which would be considered a remarkable home-field advantage except that, well . . . the Coliseum really doesn't provide much of an advantage. More likely it's simply a reflection of the quality of the teams that USC has produced over the years.

Fans in the Coliseum generally are a comfortable distance away from the players, and sound easily escapes the seating area. And as hard as it is to admit, the Coliseum is not a great place to watch a football game. Only about 25,000 seats rest between the goal lines—it was even fewer before the track was removed, and fourteen rows of seats were added more than a decade ago—and some of the others are so far away from the action that you might feel like a spectator watching the other spectators there.

City officials tried to dress up the Coliseum, making $15 million worth of renovations in 1993 and adding a new press box two years later. But more modern facilities, especially the new football-only stadiums around the NFL, are much more fan friendly. What the Coliseum lacks in intimacy and amenities, however, it more than makes up for in tradition.

USC Home Fields

The first football game in USC history in 1888 likely was played on a campus field adjoining Jefferson Avenue. From 1888 through 1922, the Trojans played at a variety of homesites. Then they moved into the Coliseum permanently with their second game of the 1923 season. Here is Troy's record on the fields they've called home:

Field	W	L	T	Pct	Seasons
Los Angeles Coliseum	400	122	27	.744	1923–2004
USC Campus	58	10	5	.829	1888–1923
Rose Bowl	23	9	0	.719	1922–2003
Fiesta Park	12	8	2	.591	1897–1916
Prager Park	4	2	0	.667	1903
Tournament Park	4	0	0	1.000	1918–21
Athletic Park	0	3	1	.125	1895–98
Washington Park	0	3	0	.000	1915–17
Chutes Park	0	1	1	.250	1900

Note: Rose Bowl figures do not include UCLA home games against USC.

The grand peristyle end of the stadium holds the Olympic torch, a reminder of the 1932 and 1984 games. And so many dramatic moments in USC history have occurred at the Coliseum that any edge the Trojans may have comes from that mystique.

Crowds at the Coliseum, like at almost all sporting events in Southern California, generally are a genteel sort not often given to fanaticism. But old-timers say there have been a handful of times that the venerable stadium has really rocked.

The first was in 1964. More than 83,000 fans flocked to the Coliseum to watch the underdog Trojans host top-ranked and undefeated Notre Dame at the close of the regular season. The Irish entered the game 9–0 and needed only a victory to secure the national championship. They appeared to be well on their way when they jumped out to a 17–0 lead at halftime.

But the Trojans battled back to within 4 points, then got the ball with one last chance to win. On fourth down from the 15 yard line and less than two minutes to go, quarterback Craig Fertig called "84-X Delay" in the huddle. Flanker Rod Sherman, who told head coach John McKay on the sidelines that he could beat his man, did just that and caught the ball at the goal line for the winning touchdown in Troy's 20–17 triumph.

Sherman said the noise level was unbelievable. And nearly two decades later, Fertig said he'd heard it that loud in the Coliseum only one other time since: at the 1974 USC–Notre Dame game.

That was the year the sixth-ranked Trojans erased a 24–0 deficit late in the first half to win 55–24. They scored 55 points in seventeen minutes of playing time and sent the crowd into a

The Trojan Marching Band is a welcome sight to USC fans. Joe Robbins

frenzy. Video from the game is memorable for the way the shaky cameras caught the Coliseum crowd literally jumping up and down in the stands.

More recently the fans at the USC-California game in 2004 produced a wall of noise that helped keep the top-ranked Trojans on the road to their second consecutive national championship. Some 90,000 fans—the largest crowd to attend a USC home game against anyone other than Notre Dame or UCLA in more than half a century—turned out to see the Trojans host the seventh-ranked Bears. California was the last team to have beaten Troy, which happened in a triple-overtime game in Berkeley in 2003. USC had won thirteen games since.

The Bears looked as if they might pull off another upset when they drove to the Trojans' 9 yard line in the final moments while trailing just 23–17. But, spurred by a raucous crowd, USC's defense stiffened. After an incompletion, a sack, and two more passes that fell to the ground, the Trojan winning streak had reached fourteen.

In 1981 top-ranked USC hosted number-two Oklahoma in the Coliseum. In one of the rare times that a one-versus-two matchup lived up to the hype, the Sooners carried a 24–21 lead late into the fourth quarter. But on their final drive, the Trojans marched from their 22 yard line to Oklahoma's 7. On second down, quarterback John Mazur's pass to a wide-open Marcus Allen in the end zone inadvertently was batted down by Fred Cornwell, who thought the ball was intended for him.

But on the next play, Cornwell made up for it. Mazur scrambled away from pressure and lofted a 7-yard scoring toss to the tight end in the left corner of the end zone with just 2 seconds left. USC won 28–24. It was the first time I had ever been on the floor of the Coliseum during a game. When Cornwell made his catch, the crowd erupted. It felt as if a massive earthquake had rocked the Coliseum.

In 1994 a massive earthquake literally did rock the Coliseum and the rest of surrounding Los Angeles. At 4:30 A.M. on January 17, the 6.7-magnitude Northridge earthquake struck.

The Coliseum suffered extensive damage and underwent a major renovation that cost $93 million. But the stadium was ready in time for the start of the 1994 season on September 3. Robinson's thirteenth-ranked Trojans beat number twenty-three Washington 24–17 in a rare conference game to open the year. Shawn Walters's 3-yard touchdown run midway through the fourth quarter won it.

In recent years, USC has been unbeatable at the Coliseum. Six opposing teams tried and failed to win there in 2003. Six more came and went the next year. In fact by the end of the 2004 season, the Trojans had forged a twenty-one-game winning string at home (with four of the victories coming by shutout). It was the longest streak in more than eight decades of history at the stadium.

The Thundering Herd

If you think it's tough being a head coach in contemporary college football's win-or-else environment, consider the plight of USC's "Gloomy Gus" Henderson in the mid-1920s.

Henderson won a school-record 86.5 percent of his games in his six seasons at Troy, but he was not brought back for the 1925 season. The big reason he was not retained was his inability to beat California, which boasted the premier college football program on the West Coast at the time. Henderson was 45–2 against everybody but California; he was 0–5 against the Bears.

Gloomy Gus, nicknamed because of his penchant for building up Trojan opponents while lamenting his own team's chances, took over a young program in 1919 and helped turn it into a force. But it wasn't until after the arrival of coach Howard Jones in 1925 that USC overtook Bay Area rivals California and Stanford and became a national power of note. Jones's teams, known collectively as the "Thundering Herd," won national championships in 1928, 1931, 1932, and 1939 and featured an array of colorful characters.

Ironically Jones was not USC's first choice to succeed Henderson; Knute Rockne was. And Rockne apparently was interested, in large part because his wife encouraged the move to sunny Southern California. But in the end the legendary Irish coach decided to stay in South Bend. (More than seventy-five years later Pete Carroll, another coach who wasn't Troy's first choice, turned out to be one of the best in USC history.)

Before heading back to the Irish sidelines, though, Rockne did USC a big favor: He recommended the former coach at Iowa for the job. Howard Jones had earned Rockne's respect when his Hawkeyes had upset the heavily favored Irish 10–7 in a game in 1921. Iowa's win put a halt to Notre Dame's twenty-two game unbeaten streak.

Gloomy Gus Henderson and Howard Jones were as different as night and day. Henderson was gregarious; Jones was reserved. Where Henderson was close to his players, Jones was aloof. Henderson could not beat California; Jones did it on his first try.

Special Skill

Elmer "Gloomy Gus" Henderson and Howard "Headman" Jones may have had disparate personalities, but they were alike in at least one respect: Neither man swore.

Henderson, the man "who put the Trojans on the map," according to Gordon Campbell (a halfback who played for Gloomy Gus from 1921 to 1923), had a simple solution when he felt his team needed a good tongue-lashing. He got someone else to do it.

"You know, he didn't cuss so he had an assistant do the cussing for him," former guard Brice Taylor told Harley Tinkham of the *Los Angeles Herald-Examiner* after Henderson's death at age seventy-six in 1965. "Honest. Whenever he got to the boiling point, he'd just call on his assistant, and he'd pour it on us."

The win came in Jones's second year, in 1926. The Trojans were coming off an 11–2 season in Jones's first year and took a 4–0 squad north to meet the Bears in Berkeley. USC dominated, winning 27–0 and serving notice that there was a new star on the rise in the Pacific Coast Conference.

USC had joined the prestigious PCC in 1922, a move the school believed would put it on a par with the bigger programs to the north. But even after finally overtaking California in 1926, it was another couple of years before Troy could overcome an additional hurdle with Stanford.

The Trojans had beaten Stanford repeatedly on Henderson's watch, but Pop Warner's Indians were a powerful squad in the mid-1920s, and they downed USC in 1925 and 1926, while tying in 1927—an outcome that cost Troy a Rose Bowl berth.

Jones's revenge came in 1928. Warner entered the game with his team on a roll, having dumped its four collegiate opponents by an average margin of more than 36 points a game, including back-to-back 47–0 routs of Idaho and Fresno State. But Jones devised his famous "quick-mix" scheme to stop the Indians in their tracks, 10–0.

Quick mix meant getting into Stanford's face right away and mixing it up—taking the action to the opponent instead of sitting back and letting Warner's bigger and heavier players dictate the play. It hardly sounds revolutionary today, but it was a bold approach for the era.

After Jones's first victory over Warner, the Trojans never looked back. They capped a 9–0–1 season (the tie was a scoreless battle in Berkeley against California) by dominating Notre Dame 27–14 at the Coliseum to win their first national championship.

As the years went on, Jones's teams no longer had to be worried about giving size away to any of its opponents. Soon the Trojans were bigger (and better) than most teams. And they became known as the Thundering Herd because of the way they ran over opponents.

They say a football team takes on the personality of its coach, and that was certainly true of the Thundering Herd. The Trojans of the Howard Jones era were straightforward, no-nonsense, 3- (or 4- or 5- or more) yards-and-a-cloud-of-dust football teams.

More often than not, they ran basic plays from a Single Wing formation. And more often than not, opponents were powerless to stop them.

Jones was a straight-laced taskmaster who didn't swear or drink, and he expected his players to be as disciplined as he was,

Head coach Howard Jones helped put Trojan football on the national map. AP

at least on the football field. His basic plays succeeded because he emphasized the basics—everyone had a job to do, and everyone had to do it well. That approach made him as successful as other, more famous coaches of the time, such as Rockne and Amos Alonzo Stagg, but in some respects he was more reminiscent of a coach of a later era—Vince Lombardi.

Jones made it a priority to beat the California teams, and he did, including a 5–0–2 mark against USC's newest in-state rival, UCLA. But he also directed the Trojans to several victories on the national stage, the biggest being their famous 16–14 victory over Notre Dame in South Bend in 1931.

After USC rallied from a 14–0, fourth-quarter deficit to beat the Irish 16–14 on Johnny Baker's field goal in the final minute, the Trojans celebrated in style. They were decked out in bowler hats by a Chicago haberdashery and returned home to a ticker-tape parade, the likes of which had not been seen before, outside of Manhattan.

More than 300,000 fans lined the streets in downtown Los Angeles to welcome the conquering heroes. Office workers tossed torn up pages from the phone book and shredded stationery out the windows, and people crowded the sidewalks to get a glimpse of Jones and Baker and the rest of the team. "I had never seen such a crowd in my life," tackle Ernie Smith said. Later the game film was shown at a downtown movie theater, and it drew big crowds for weeks.

USC hadn't fielded an All-America player before Jones arrived. But it is an indication of the measure of national respect that the program achieved on his watch that the Trojans had twenty-four first-teamers from 1925 to 1940.

USC (in the dark jerseys) and California do battle in 1932. AP

Guard Brice Taylor was Troy's first All-American in 1925. Some of the others—Morley Drury, Garrett Arbelbide, Orv Mohler, Erny Pinckert, Gaius Shaver, "Cotton" Warburton, and Grenville Lansdell—are among the most distinguished players in school history.

Even the names themselves sound regal. Jim Murray, the late, great columnist of the *Los Angeles Times*, once wrote that USC got its backfields from "the pages of the Brönte Sisters or Thackeray or Macaulay. They are the stuff of myths."

Jones was a coach singularly committed to football, a coach who reportedly would lose his way home because he was so wrapped up in thoughts about his sport. But he also was fiercely loyal to his players.

In 1927 Jones sent Morley Drury, the "Noblest Trojan of Them All," to the locker room with the game well in hand in the fourth quarter of USC's 33–13 victory over Washington on Homecoming Day at the Coliseum. But he sent him across the field, instead of along the sidelines and behind the end zone. It was Drury's last game (he ran for 183 yards and scored 3 touchdowns in the rout), and Jones wanted one of the most beloved Trojans to get a standing ovation from the 60,000 fans in attendance. He did.

Even though they lost two games, Jones's 1929 team was a powerful, physical squad that was the first to be known as the Thundering Herd. The name came from a Zane Grey novel (and a motion picture based on the book) with the same title. The 1929 Trojans won ten games, outscored their opponents 492–69, and walloped Pittsburgh 47–14 in the Rose Bowl.

Baker's famous field goal propelled USC to its second national title in 1931, and Troy repeated in 1932 while allowing only 13 points all season en route to ten consecutive wins.

Jones's last great team was in 1939. The Trojans tied Oregon 7–7 in the opener, then reeled off seven consecutive victories, including a 20–12 win at number-seven Notre Dame. The Irish were the only team to score more than seven points against USC all year. The Trojans ended the regular season with a scoreless tie against UCLA. In the Rose Bowl, USC scored the first points allowed by Tennessee all year and beat the Volunteers 14–0.

In 1940 Jones's final team lost four of its last five games and finished just 3–4–2. But he never got a chance to bounce back

Barry Good

Sam Barry succeeded Howard Jones as the Trojans' football coach in 1941, but he was primarily known as USC's baseball coach. When Troy needed a new coach after Jones died suddenly with a new season on the horizon, they turned to Barry, who did his best to hold the Trojans together during a 2–6–1 season.

It may have been too much to ask of anyone, even the man who helped jump-start USC's grand tradition in baseball. Barry became the school's baseball coach in 1930 and was an immediate hit. He led the Trojans to fifteen victories in seventeen decisions against college teams and to their first California Intercollegiate Baseball Association title. In his twelve full seasons at the helm, Barry guided Troy to five CIBA championships and compiled a record of 133–54–2 against college opponents.

In 1942 and again from 1946 until his death in 1950, Barry and the soon-to-be-legendary Rod Dedeaux were co–head coaches. (Sam was in the Navy from 1943 to 1945.) In 1948 the duo helped the Trojans win the first of their record twelve national championships in baseball.

from such a disappointing year. Two months before the start of the 1941 season, Howard Jones died of a heart attack at age fifty-five.

After his death, USC went through several head coaches, trying to recapture the magic that the "Headman" brought to the

USC Coaching Records (pre-1960)

	W	L	T	Pct
Henry Goddard, Frank Suffel (1888)	2	0	0	1.000
Lewis Freeman (1897)	5	1	0	.833
Clair Tappaan (1901)	0	1	1	.250
John Walker (1903)	4	2	0	.667
Harvey Holmes (1904–7)	19	5	3	.759
William Traeger (1908)	3	1	1	.700
Dean Cromwell (1909–10, 1916–18)	21	8	6	.686
Ralph Glaze (1914–15)	7	7	0	.500
Elmer Henderson (1919–24)	45	7	0	.865
Howard Jones (1925–40)	121	36	13	.750
Sam Barry (1941)	2	6	1	.278
Jeff Cravath (1942–50)	54	28	8	.644
Jess Hill (1951–56)	45	17	1	.722
Don Clark (1957–59)	13	16	1	.450

program. Sam Barry was thrust into the position on an emergency basis in 1941, and Troy managed to win only two games.

The next season, the Trojans turned to one of their own for the first time for their head coach. The school hired Jeff Cravath, a center on Jones's first team in 1925 and the senior captain of the 1926 squad. After graduation Cravath spent two seasons as an assistant to Jones, then had stints as the head coach at Denver University, Chaffey Junior College, and the University of San Francisco. His 1941 Dons featured an explosive offense that utilized the revolutionary new T-formation.

Cravath brought the T to USC and, although he never came close to matching his mentor's record of national championships, he had a large degree of success. Under Cravath, Troy earned four Rose Bowl berths in the five-season span from 1943 to 1947. His 1943 team upset twelfth-ranked Washington 29–0 in the only Rose Bowl played between two West Coast teams (because of wartime travel restrictions), and the 1944 squad drubbed number-twelve Tennessee 25–0. That was Cravath's best team: USC finished the season 8–0–2 and ranked seventh in the nation.

In 1951 Jess Hill succeeded Cravath as coach. Another former Trojan, Hill starred in baseball, track, and football for USC in the late 1920s. After a brief career in baseball's major leagues (he batted .289 in three seasons with the New York Yankees, Washington Senators, and Philadelphia Athletics), he embarked on a coaching career that landed him Troy's top track-and-field job in 1949. The Trojans won back-to-back national championships in his first two years at the helm, and Hill took over the football program the next year.

Hill never had a losing season in six years as Troy's coach. His 1952 squad went 10–1 and beat Wisconsin 7–0 in the Rose Bowl to give the Pacific Coast Conference its first victory over the Big Ten since the two leagues agreed in 1947 to send their respective champions to Pasadena on New Year's Day. Two years later Hill's seventeenth-ranked Trojans lost to number-one Ohio State 20–7 in the rain and mud in the Rose Bowl.

Don Clark, who played three seasons for Cravath in the 1940s, took over in 1957. He coached for three seasons before giving way to an unknown named John McKay in 1960 — and the longest sustained stretch of success in the Trojans' illustrious gridiron history was just on the horizon.

From Tailback U to Quarterback U

USC head coach John McKay didn't invent the I-formation. But he certainly put the *i* in Heisman. McKay's obsession with perfecting the I—countless diagrams scribbled on yellow notepads while sitting in the den of his home, a cigar in his mouth and a black-and-white Western playing on the television screen—helped produce two Heisman Trophy winners and win four national championships in his sixteen-year tenure at Troy from 1960 to 1975. And it helped the school earn a moniker for which it became known across the nation: Tailback U.

While McKay was not the first to adopt the I-formation, as he is often credited, he did refine it and make one critical adjustment: He had his deep back standing up in the backfield.

Other college coaches, such as Maryland and Florida State's Tom Nugent, had utilized the I before. McKay himself said he saw Don Coryell implement the formation while coaching junior college football in Washington. But McKay's predecessors always had the deep back in a normal three-point stance. The Trojans' coach, meanwhile, remembered his days as a Single Wing tailback, when he ran from a standing start and got a good, early look at the defense. So in his I-formation, McKay positioned his tailback standing, with his hands on his knees and with an excellent vantage point of the opponent. (Of course, McKay stood only 5'9" inches and could use the extra advantage; then again, his first great tailback, Mike Garrett, was just 5'9", also.)

McKay initially began running the I in 1961, though the Trojans most often shifted out of it before the ball was snapped. Once he recognized the myriad options that the I gave him, he began using it more and more. Pretty soon, USC was running virtually every play from the I.

And pretty soon the Trojans had their first Heisman Trophy winner. Mike Garrett, who was built more like a bowling ball than a Trojan horse, was not a typical USC I-formation tailback. On the other hand there was no prototype at the time, because Garrett was the first among the litany of the Trojans' great I-formation tailbacks. "I'm proud of that," Garrett said.

He countered his small size with amazing instincts, raw running power, and heart. "Nobody ever got more out of his ability," McKay said. The coach recognized that early and made the sophomore his starter in 1963. In fall scrimmages, he ran his new tailback into the line repeatedly. "Iron Mike" withstood the punishment. "I've found my guy," McKay thought.

Garrett's tireless work ethic led to a long-standing tradition among Trojan tailbacks. At practice, instead of stopping after he broke through the line, he would keep running hard downfield, 30 to 40 yards. "He gives 100 percent every game and every minute of practice," McKay said.

Another tradition that started under McKay in the 1960s was the "bag drill." Garrett—and all subsequent USC tailbacks—ran a gauntlet through various assistant coaches standing in two lines just a few yards wide. The coaches threw heavy bags, the kind used in blocking drills, at the running back's feet and shoulders from both directions. It was a bruising drill that helped runners with their balance, vision, and power.

Balance was one of Garrett's strengths. He had a splay-footed running style that may have looked funny to opposing players, but they soon found it was no laughing matter. "He changes direction almost full stride," said one vanquished opponent.

Garrett ranked seventh nationally with 883 rushing yards in 1963 and was sixth with 948 yards in 1964 before becoming the first USC player to lead the nation in rushing with 1,440 yards in 1965. He was an All-America selection his junior and senior seasons, set an NCAA career rushing record with 3,221 yards, and easily outdistanced Tulsa end Howard Twilley in the Heisman Trophy balloting.

Tailback Tradition

In the seventeen-season span from 1965—the year that Mike Garrett first broke the 1,000-yard barrier—through 1981, USC produced fourteen 1,000-yard rushers among its tailbacks. Here are the Trojans' year-by-year rushing leaders those seasons:

Year	Player	Yards
1965	Mike Garrett	1,440
1966	Don McCall	560
1967	O. J. Simpson	1,543
1968	O. J. Simpson	1,880
1969	Clarence Davis	1,351
1970	Clarence Davis	972
1971	Lou Harris	801
1972	Anthony Davis	1,191
1973	Anthony Davis	1,112
1974	Anthony Davis	1,421
1975	Ricky Bell	1,957
1976	Ricky Bell	1,433
1977	Charles White	1,478
1978	Charles White	1,859
1979	Charles White	2,050
1980	Marcus Allen	1,563
1981	Marcus Allen	2,427

About all that was missing from Garrett's resume was a Rose Bowl appearance. He came agonizingly close. In 1963 a loss in the mud at Washington was the only blemish on the Trojans'

conference slate. In 1964 USC tied Oregon State for the conference title, then closed the season with an upset of number-one
ranked Notre Dame. But AAWU representatives voted the
Beavers to the Rose Bowl. And in 1965 the sixth-ranked Trojans
were in line for a trip to Pasadena until seventh-ranked UCLA
rallied for a 20–16 victory in their annual matchup. Garrett did
all he could in that one, carrying the ball 40 times for 210 yards.

Two years later O. J. Simpson arrived as a junior college
transfer from City College of San Francisco. Simpson had worn
braces on his legs as a toddler, stricken by disease, but by the time
he arrived at USC, he stood a strapping 6'2" and weighed 207
pounds. He combined that size with a sprinter's speed and didn't
seem to slow down under the weight of a helmet and shoulder
pads.

In his second game for Troy, he carried the ball 30 times for
164 yards in a 17–13 victory over fifth-ranked Texas. That was a
harbinger of things to come. He had 190 yards rushing in a win
at Michigan State that vaulted USC to the top spot in the
national polls, then 163 yards against Stanford, and 169 in a 24–7
rout of number-five Notre Dame.

In later years Irish coach Ara Parseghian lamented that O. J.
would walk back to the huddle as if exhausted or burdened by
some unbearable weight. "You'd think, now we've got him,"
Parseghian said. "Then he'd take the ball and run 40 yards."

Invariably, Simpson would get stronger as the game went on,
prompting McKay to say on more than one occasion, "In the
fourth quarter, O. J. got faster—and I got smarter."

O. J. narrowly missed winning the Heisman Trophy after running for 1,543 yards as a junior in 1967, but there was never a

doubt in 1968: Simpson won by the largest margin in history. He began the season by amassing 367 all-purpose yards (including 236 on the ground) in a 29–20 victory at number-sixteen Minnesota, and he never slowed down. After rushing for an NCAA-record 1,709 yards in the regular season (he added another 171 yards against Ohio State in the Rose Bowl), O. J. carried every region in the voting and earned first-place votes on 855 of the Downtown Athletic Club's 1,200 ballots. The next closest, Purdue's Leroy Keyes, had just 49 first-place votes.

One by one, the great tailbacks followed at USC: Clarence Davis, Anthony Davis, Ricky Bell, Charles White, Marcus Allen. All of them were All-Americans.

Clarence Davis rushed for 1,351 yards and helped the Trojans go undefeated in 1969 at 10–0–1. The late Mal Florence, who wrote *The Trojan Heritage* in 1980, called Davis the "forgotten" tailback. It could have been as much for Clarence's quiet demeanor as it was for his spot in the pantheon of USC greats between superstars O. J. Simpson and Anthony Davis.

Clarence Davis, who helped USC beat Michigan 10–3 in the Rose Bowl on New Year's Day 1970, had the best game of his eight-year NFL career on the same field in January of 1977. He ran for a career-best 137 yards on just 16 carries to lead the Oakland Raiders to a 32–14 victory over the Minnesota Vikings in Super Bowl XI.

Clarence was a guard in high school, but McKay knew a great tailback when he saw one. It was the same for Anthony Davis, who was the Los Angeles city player of the year while a quarterback at San Fernando High School.

Anthony Davis began his varsity career at Troy in 1972 as a backup to Rod McNeill. He didn't become a starter until the

Tailback Charles White poses with his Heisman Trophy in 1979. AP

eighth game, but he still managed to surpass 1,000 yards on the ground for the first of three consecutive seasons.

While Clarence Davis was quiet and unobtrusive, there was nothing understated about the boisterous and flashy Anthony Davis. His trademark touchdown celebration on his knees still torments Notre Dame fans after all these years.

Ricky Bell followed Anthony Davis and earned unanimous All-America honors in back-to-back seasons of 1975 and 1976. As a junior in 1975, he set a school record (since broken) by running for 1,957 yards. The next year he set a single-game mark that still stands when he ran for 347 yards on 51 carries in a 23–14 victory in Seattle over Washington State.

Anthony Davis and Bell narrowly missed winning the Heisman Trophy in 1974 and 1976, respectively, each finishing second in the balloting. It was Charles White who won USC's third Heisman in 1979.

A native of Los Angeles's San Fernando Valley who grew up watching Garrett, Simpson, and the other Trojan tailbacks, White always knew he wanted to go to USC. Though he was known for his breakaway speed and stood only 5'11" tall, White was one of the toughest and most durable USC backs ever. "He could play a doubleheader if he wanted to," head coach John Robinson once said.

White often packed two games' worth of carries into one. In a 42–23 victory at ninth-ranked Notre Dame his senior season, he ran the ball 44 times for 261 yards. The next week he lugged the ball 44 times again to help beat California. At season's end he had carried 332 times for 2,050 yards (including 247 yards against Ohio State in the Rose Bowl), and he led the nation by averaging 180.3 yards per game during the regular season.

Believe it or not, those figures paled in comparison to the statistics that Marcus Allen generated just two years later. Allen, who arrived on the USC campus as a defensive back and primarily served as a blocking back for White as a sophomore in 1979, was shifted to tailback in 1980. He ran for 1,563 yards—an excellent figure, but not good enough for Coliseum fans who had become accustomed to the sight of Trojan tailbacks atop the NCAA rushing list. Allen's 4.4 yards per carry average also was far less than White's 6.2, and there were cries to move the former San Diego high school star back to fullback his senior season to make room for young Todd Spencer or Michael Harper. Fortunately the only

Marcus Allen had a record-setting season in 1981. AP

vote that counted was that of head coach John Robinson. He stuck with Allen, and the results were unbelievable.

Marcus began the 1981 season by rushing for 210 yards in a 43–7 rout of Tennessee, despite sitting out much of the second half. He had 274 yards the following week against Indiana, and when he added 208 in the top-ranked Trojans' 28–24 victory over Oklahoma, it was apparent something special was going on.

Allen became the first collegiate running back to record five consecutive 200-yard games when he reached the plateau against Oregon State (233 yards) and Arizona (211). By season's end he had run for more than 200 yards in a record eight games, and he became the first college runner ever to reach 2,000 yards in the regular season, shattering the barrier with 2,342 yards (he finished with 2,427, including his Fiesta Bowl totals).

Marcus was pretty much the Trojans' offense in 1981: He led the team with 34 receptions, and he scored 23 touchdowns overall. "He can do so many things," Robinson said. "He blocks well, runs well, and catches well."

Allen was Robinson's second Heisman-winning tailback (White was the first). But when Robinson was named USC's coach in 1976, he expressed a desire to make the quarterback more prominent in the offense.

"The USC tailback is the best single position in college football," he said then. "Now we want to create a similar environment for the quarterback. We want to make the quarterback position more successful."

And Robinson was true to his word. Even with White running wild in 1979, quarterback Paul McDonald earned All-America honors that year, also, and set USC passing records. A few years later, Robinson landed one of the top prep quarterbacks in the nation in Sean Salisbury of Vista's Orange Glen High School.

By the time Salisbury was a senior, another heralded freshman began making his mark. Rodney Peete eventually finished second to Oklahoma State running back Barry Sanders in the Heisman balloting in 1988—the highest finish ever for a Trojan quarterback.

And more than a decade later, in 2002, a USC quarterback broke through to win the Heisman for the first time. Carson Palmer became the Trojans' first winner in twenty-one years (and the first from the West Coast in the same span).

Palmer, a highly recruited star out of Laguna Niguel's Santa Margarita High School, had spent four largely unremarkable years at Troy since first stepping onto campus in 1998. He appeared ready to blossom his sophomore season after leading USC to back-

Heisman Hype

Schools with the most Heisman Trophy winners (through 2004):

NOTRE DAME   7
Angelo Bertelli, QB (1943); John Lujack, QB (1947);
   Leon Hart, E (1949); John Lattner, RB (1953);
   Paul Hornung, QB (1956); John Huarte, QB (1964);
   Tim Brown, WR (1987)

USC   6
Mike Garrett, RB (1965); O. J. Simpson, RB (1968);
   Charles White, RB (1979); Marcus Allen, RB (1981);
   Carson Palmer, QB (2002); Matt Leinart, QB (2004)

OHIO STATE   6
Les Horvath, QB (1944); Vic Janowicz, RB (1950);
   Howard Cassady, RB (1955); Archie Griffin, RB (1974
   and 1975); Eddie George, RB (1995)

OKLAHOMA   4
Billy Vessels, RB (1952); Steve Owens, FB (1969);
   Billy Sims, RB (1978); Jason White, QB (2003)

ARMY   3
Doc Blanchard, FB (1945); Glenn Davis, RB (1946);
   Pete Dawkins, RB (1958)

MICHIGAN   3
Tom Harmon, RB (1940); Desmond Howard, WR (1991);
   Charles Woodson, CB (1997)

NEBRASKA   3
Johnny Rodgers, FL (1972); Mike Rozier, RB (1983);
   Eric Crouch, QB (2001)

In 2002 Carson Palmer became the first USC quarterback to win the Heisman. Joe Robbins

to-back victories at the start the year. He then helped the Trojans take a lead into the waning moments of a game at Oregon, where the Ducks were in the midst of a twenty-three-game winning streak at Autzen Stadium. But Oregon rallied to beat USC 33–30 in the final minute, and the Trojans suffered a more devastating blow when Palmer was lost for the season to a broken collarbone suffered in the second quarter, when he lowered his shoulder into a Ducks defender while fighting for extra yards on a scramble.

Palmer redshirted the year, and it eventually paid dividends. In 2002, under the tutelage of head coach Pete Carroll and quarterback guru Norm Chow, Palmer fulfilled the promise he had shown from his first game in 1998, when he came off the bench as a freshman to help USC beat Purdue to open the season.

Palmer set school records by completing 63.2 percent of his passes for 3,942 yards and 33 touchdowns, against only 10 interceptions. He guided a prolific offense that averaged 41.5 points per game in an eight-game winning streak at the end of the season. And he may have won the Heisman when he passed for a Notre Dame–opponent-record 425 yards and 4 touchdowns in a nationally televised 44–13 rout of the seventh-ranked Irish. But the most memorable play of a memorable season was a 22-yard scramble in USC's 52–21 thrashing of UCLA the week before. Palmer finished off the run by hurdling defenders near the goal line. He didn't make it into the end zone, but his whirlybird motion made highlight shows across the country and earned praise from his teammates.

By season's end, the Orange Bowl–champion Trojans may have been the country's best team, but two close losses on the road early in the year kept them from the national championship.

Pete Carroll talks things over with quarterback Matt Leinart, the 2004 Heisman Trophy winner. Joe Robbins

The title would come a year later, under a new quarterback, Matt Leinart. And a year after that, Leinart succeeded Palmer as USC's sixth Heisman Trophy winner.

Leinart passed for 3,556 yards and 38 touchdowns in his first season as a starter in 2003; they may have been even better as a junior in 2004. Though his numbers were down slightly—3,322 yards and 33 touchdowns—they came despite inexperience on the offensive line and in the wide receiver corps. Into that void, Leinart stepped up as the unquestioned leader of Troy's 13–0 team.

With two Heisman winners in three seasons, folks have begun calling USC "Quarterback U" instead of "Tailback U." Or, as Mike Garrett, the former Heisman-winning tailback and the school's athletic director, put it in New York after Leinart was named the winner of the 2004 Heisman: "USC's tradition is first and foremost about winning. If it takes a quarterback, we'll take it."

Trophy Case

Here are some other USC major award winners:

OUTLAND TROPHY
(presented since 1946 to the outstanding interior lineman in the
    United States)
Ron Yary   1967

LOMBARDI AWARD
(presented since 1970 to the top collegiate lineman who "best
    exemplifies the discipline of Vince Lombardi")
Brad Budde   1979

THORPE AWARD
(presented since 1986 to the top defensive back in the nation)
Mark Carrier   1989

BUTKUS AWARD
(presented since 1985 to the top linebacker in the nation)
Chris Claiborne   1998

But don't give up on tailbacks just yet. After producing a mere seven 1,000-yard rushers in the twenty-three seasons since Allen won the Heisman in 1981, LenDale White gained 1,103 yards on only 203 rushes (an average of 5.4 yards per carry) for Troy in 2004. And right behind was explosive, all-purpose tailback Reggie Bush. He ran for 908 yards, caught 43 passes for 511 yards, and added 913 yards on punt and kickoff returns. He joined Leinart in New York as a Heisman finalist in 2004, finishing fifth.

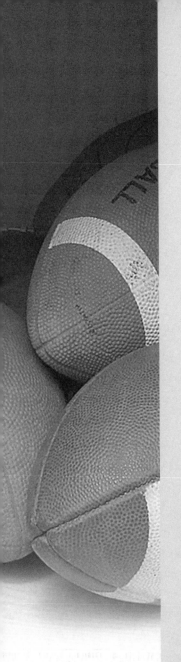

McKay
Leads
the Way

On December 15, 1959, USC president Norman Topping announced that Don Clark had resigned as the school's head football coach. Topping also announced that the new coach of the Trojans, a team that already had won several national championships, a team that had played in a dozen Rose Bowls, a team that had built a following from coast to coast was . . . John McKay.

Who? That was the collective response from USC alumni and supporters, as well as much of the Los Angeles media. In direct contrast to many contemporary coaching searches that recruited big names to come to the big-time college football programs, Topping looked no further than Clark's staff. And the man he settled on—in large part because of the recommendation of Clark himself—was a little-known assistant who had been with the Trojans for just one season.

Under the circumstances, it looked as if McKay had been brought to the university prior to the 1959 season for the purpose of settling in for a year, then taking over for Clark. But that wasn't the case. Clark, who had suffered through 1–9 and 4–5–1 seasons in 1957 and 1958 after Pacific Coast Conference sanctions hit the school hard, had turned things around quickly, going 8–2 in his final season. USC, in fact, won its first eight games in 1959 and rose as high as number four in the Associated Press poll before its offense stalled in losses of 10–3 to UCLA and 16–6 to Notre Dame to close the year.

Clark's job was secure, at least for the time being. But his brother, who was running the family's industrial-sized laundry business, was in ill health and had been pressuring Don to take over. Clark, who was only in his late thirties and needed to feed a family of seven kids, realized there was more money to be made—and more long-term job security—in his family's business. So he retired from coaching.

Clark had no second thoughts about going into business. The company, Prudential Overall Supply, has grown to about 2,000 employees with annual sales of more than $100 million. Nor did he have any second thoughts about turning over the program to McKay, who himself was only thirty-six years old at the time. The

John McKay being carried off the field after a perfect season in 1962. AP

former Oregon end, who had mulled an offer to coach in the NFL as an assistant for the 1960 season, was startled at his sudden good fortune. He was the first coach since Sam Barry in 1941 who hadn't gone to USC.

If there was a honeymoon period for Johnny McKay, as the newspapers initially called him, it was over quickly. The Trojans entered McKay's first game in 1960 ranked number six in the country and a prohibitive 18-point favorite at home over Oregon State. But USC fumbled 5 times, losing 4 of them, and mustered fewer than 200 yards total offense. The Beavers, coached by Tommy Prothro (the future UCLA and Los Angeles Rams coach) won easily, 14–0. The Trojans "couldn't block, tackle, or hold on to the ball," read the next day's *Los Angeles Times*. Other than that, as McKay might have said, they weren't too bad.

Things got only marginally better the next week, when visiting TCU edged USC 7–6. The Trojans were foiled by a missed extra point and a missed field goal try. "We have an overrated team," McKay said in a classic understatement.

USC, in fact, had been named the nation's top team in *Playboy* magazine's college football preview. It simply proved that "*Playboy* knows a lot more about the female formation than the T-formation," McKay said.

The Trojans went on to finish the season 4–6, with a 17–6 upset of eleventh-ranked UCLA late in the year being the biggest win. "It only saved my job," McKay said. A 4–5–1 season that included a 1-point loss to top-ranked Iowa followed before McKay produced his first winner in 1962.

USC began the 1962 season unranked but quickly vaulted into the top ten with a 14–7 upset of number-eight Duke. The

Funny Man

Some of former USC head coach John McKay's most memorable one-liners:

- When asked by a reporter if he was utilizing workhorse running back O. J. Simpson too much: "Why? The ball isn't heavy. Besides, he doesn't belong to a union."

- When a USC player fielded the opening kickoff in a game against Notre Dame at South Bend, took two steps, and fell flat on his face: "My God, they shot him!"

- When warned by the officials before another game in South Bend that he had to come onto the field before Notre Dame's team or risk a 2–0 forfeit: "That would be the best deal we've ever gotten in this stadium."

- On the importance of intensity to a football team: "Intensity is a lot of guys who run fast."

- After USC's historic 51–0 loss to Notre Dame in 1966: "I told our players there were 700 million Chinese who didn't even know the game was played. The next week, I got five letters from China, saying, 'What happened?'"

- On one of his favorite targets, sportswriters: "I said on my television show that they didn't know a quarterback from a banana stand, and someone sent me a crate of bananas. This week, I'm going to say most writers don't know a quarterback from a Mercedes."

Trojans didn't lose, finishing off an 11–0 season by beating Wisconsin in the Rose Bowl for their first unbeaten and untied season since 1932.

McKay never had another losing year. His 1967, 1972, and 1974 teams joined the 1962 squad as national champions. In all, he compiled a record of 127–40–8 in sixteen seasons at USC. Three of his teams went undefeated; three others lost only one game. He took eight teams to the Rose Bowl.

McKay could be moody, aloof, and sarcastic, but he also could be charming, thought provoking, and downright funny.

He was a delegator, one who came up with the game plans but left the hands-on teaching to his assistants. He communicated with the team's head manager but rarely talked with any of his other aides. And he often would cruise around the practice field in a golf cart or watch from a tower above Howard Jones Field on campus, a habit that further separated him from the players.

Some players openly expressed their dislike for McKay in later years, citing his distant demeanor. Such criticism bothered McKay—not so much that he needed to be liked by his players. He felt the best way to help them develop into young men was not by getting chummy with them but by setting a good example.

Still, other players remembered their old coach with great respect. "Coach was an autocrat," former USC quarterback Pat Haden wrote in the *Los Angeles Times* following McKay's death at age seventy-seven in 2001. "His players always knew there was only one decision maker. But he loved his players, even if he did not show it with outward signs of affection."

McKay was called a "riverboat gambler" by the press, because he refused to settle for a tie late in games, no matter how

A happy John McKay hugs
Trojans tailback Mike Garrett.
AP

important they were. He gave an early indication of that in the third week of the 1961 season, his second as a head coach. After drawing within a point of top-rated Iowa with just 48 seconds left, the unranked Trojans elected to go for two. It failed, and the Hawkeyes survived, 35–34.

When McKay eschewed a tie, and the Trojans failed on a two-point conversion attempt late in the 1967 Rose Bowl against Purdue, a reporter asked him if the players wanted to go for the win. McKay said that he believed they all wanted it but also that "I didn't have time to hold a convention."

Such wit most often was described as acerbic, and McKay's barbs could be directed at anyone: opponents, media, fans, players, even himself. "I've checked my heart," he once told his wife, Corky, after a particularly close game. "I don't have one."

It was Corky who helped persuade her husband to leave Oregon for the USC assistant's job in 1959. A former Trojan coed, she lived and died with Trojan football. "People say football is a game of emotion," McKay liked to say. "Well, Corky is the most emotional person I know. And she can't play football worth a damn."

One year, Corky expressed relief that the USC–UCLA game was over with because she hadn't slept the whole week leading up to the big game. "Why not?" the coach asked. "I never intended to play you, anyway."One family member McKay did play was his son Johnny. The younger McKay, an excellent pass catcher who led the Trojans with 34 receptions as a senior in 1974, really had to prove he belonged on the field to forestall any charges of nepotism. Of course, the coach didn't help when he said he had an edge in recruiting the split end "because I slept with his mother."

McKay initially spurned several offers to coach in the pros, including one from one of the Coliseum's other tenants, the Los Angeles Rams. According to his book *A Coach's Story*, cowritten with Jim Perry, he also politely declined an overture from Paul "Bear" Bryant to succeed the legendary coach at Alabama.

In the early 1970s McKay had been tempted to take a multi-million-dollar offer to become the head coach and general manager of the New England Patriots, but it wasn't until late in the 1975 season that he decided to make the jump to the NFL, taking over the expansion franchise Tampa Bay Buccaneers.

The coach broke the news to his players at a team meeting in late October as they were about to leave for the airport and a flight to the Bay Area for a game against California. The Trojans were 7–0 and ranked number four in the country at the time, but the stunned players never had a chance against the Bears. Cal, which featured a powerful offense led by quarterback Joe Roth, running back Chuck Muncie, and wide receiver Wesley Walker, amassed 477 total yards and won 28–14.

USC went on to lose its next three games before sending McKay away with a 20–0 rout of number-two Texas A & M in the Liberty Bowl. It was the first time the Trojans were eligible to play in a bowl without winning their conference.

McKay's early, undermanned teams struggled badly in Tampa, setting an NFL record for futility by losing its first twenty-six games. After one particularly poor exhibition, a reporter asked McKay about his team's execution. "I'm in favor of it," the coach snapped.

By 1979, though, McKay—relying largely on the running of former Trojan tailback Ricky Bell and linebacker Richard

Sweet Sixteen

Year-by-year with John McKay in his sixteen seasons as coach of the Trojans:

Year	Record	Bowl
1960	4–6–0	
1961	4–5–1	
1962	11–0–0	Rose
1963	7–3–0	
1964	7–3–0	
1965	7–2–1	
1966	7–4–0	Rose
1967	10–1–0	Rose
1968	9–1–1	Rose
1969	10–0–1	Rose
1970	6–4–1	
1971	6–4–1	
1972	12–0–0	Rose
1973	9–2–1	Rose
1974	10–1–1	Rose
1975	8–4–0	Liberty
Totals	127–40–8	

Wood—had led the Buccaneers to a division championship and the NFC Championship Game.

Meanwhile, back at USC, the Trojans had plucked another Oregonian from a former staff of McKay's to succeed him. John

Robinson, the offensive coordinator for Troy's 1972 and 1974 national champions before becoming an assistant to the Oakland Raiders coach John Madden in 1975, took over as USC head coach in 1976.

Like his predecessor, Robinson was a bright, young offensive thinker with a terrific sense of humor. But he was generally more at ease with players and the media than McKay had been, and his humor was less cutting and often self-deprecating.

On the field, the Trojans didn't miss a beat. Though Robinson's debut was a disaster—"They probably wanted to get rid of me right then," he said of a 46–25 thrashing by Missouri at the Coliseum—USC rolled off twelve straight wins after that. The season ended with consecutive victories over number-two UCLA (24–14), number-thirteen Notre Dame (17–13), and number-two Michigan in the Rose Bowl (14–6). Only Pittsburgh, which went undefeated with Heisman Trophy running back Tony Dorsett carrying the load, blocked the Trojans' path to the national championship. USC had to settle for number two.

Robinson soon got his national championship, though. After guiding the Trojans to a victory in the Bluebonnet Bowl in 1977, Robinson led his 1978 team to a 24–14 upset of top-ranked Alabama at Legion Field in Birmingham in the season's third game. Only a 20–7 loss at Arizona State marred USC's 12–1 season, and a 17–10 victory over number-five Michigan in the Rose Bowl lifted the Trojans to the top of the UPI coaches poll. The Associated Press national champ? Alabama, the same team the Trojans had soundly defeated in a hostile environment.

Robinson's initial stint at USC lasted from 1976 to 1982. His overall record was a remarkable 67–14–2 before he stepped down to take a post as a university vice president. He did not last long in the desk job, resigning soon after to coach in the NFL. Assistant Ted Tollner, an offensive-minded coach who cut his teeth at pass-happy San Diego State and BYU, was hired to replace him as head coach.

The first game of Tollner's coaching career, against Florida in the Coliseum, offered little indication of the travails on the horizon; then at the same time it offered one massive clue at the very end.

Head coach Charley Pell's Florida team, which featured quarterback Wayne Peace, was on the verge of becoming a national power and entered the season ranked eighteenth in the country. Florida led 19–13 when the Trojans moved to the Gators' 40 yard line with time for one more play. Quarterback Sean Salisbury's pass fell incomplete as time expired, and it appeared that Tollner had become the fourth consecutive USC coach (after Clark, McKay, and Robinson) to lose his opening game.

But wait! The Gators had twelve men on the field, and a game cannot end on a defensive penalty. Because the twelfth man was an active participant, the infraction was a 15-yarder. Given another chance with no time showing on the clock, Salisbury threaded a rope to a leaping Timmie Ware in the end zone. The Trojans celebrated, the crowd went wild, and Florida's players slumped. It now appeared that Tollner would become the first Trojan coach since Jess Hill in 1951 to win his first game as coach.

Wait again! The score was only tied pending the formality of the extra-point kick. But the snap was low, and holder Tim Green, the backup quarterback, yelled "Fire!"—the code word to

John Robinson coached
twice for USC.
Chris Pizzello/AP

alert the kick team that something had gone awry. Green picked up the ball, rolled out, and fired a pass that was incomplete. The game ended up tied at 19–19. No one was quite sure how to act after the bizarre ending. The Trojans would have lost except for the penalty that gave them a second chance . . . but they certainly should have won when all it took after that was an extra point.

The irony is that there was no reason for Green to have yelled "Fire!" He did the right thing under normal circumstances, of course, but it was easy to see that the stunned Gators had given up. They were so dejected that they hadn't even bothered to rush on the extra point, conceding almost certain defeat. Green had plenty of time to pick up the bad snap and place it down.

Unfortunately, the late-game heroics were less a portent of things to come than the extra-point fiasco. Several weeks later, during a 27–6 loss to an unranked Notre Dame that was not even as close as the lopsided score indicated, USC took two time-outs on an extra-point try—then missed (it was a two-point attempt).

The Trojans rebounded from Tollner's 4–6–1 rookie season to win nine of their first ten games in 1984, including a 16–7 upset of number-one Washington to clinch a Rose Bowl berth. Many of the good feelings that victory generated, though, were squandered when USC inexplicably fell flat in back-to-back losses to unranked UCLA (29–10) and Notre Dame (19–7) to end the regular season. Despite a 20–17 upset of sixth-ranked Ohio State in the Rose Bowl, as well as two succeeding bowl berths, Tollner was let go following the 1986 season.

Tollner's teams were 26–20–1 overall, but just 1–7 against UCLA and Notre Dame. With that in mind, USC hired a man who knew how to win a rivalry game: Arizona's Larry Smith. Though his Arizona teams were often the underdog, Smith had considerable success against archenemy Arizona State during his seven-year tenure as the Wildcats coach. His last five Arizona teams beat the Sun Devils. In addition his 1981 squad had come to the Coliseum and spotted number-one USC a 10–0 lead, then roared back for a stunning 13–10 upset.

Smith's first USC team lost to tenth-ranked Notre Dame in South Bend but late in the season stunned number-five UCLA 17–13 to give the Trojans an unexpected Rose Bowl berth. Two more Rose Bowls followed, the last a 17–10 victory over Michigan to cap the 1989 season and hand outgoing Wolverines coach Bo Schembechler (Smith's former mentor) a loss in his last game.

The bloom quickly came off Smith's rose, however. After a 3–8 season in 1991 that included six consecutive losses—the longest in USC history—the Trojans ended the 1992 season with three straight defeats, the last an embarrassing 24–7 loss to unranked Fresno State in the short-lived Freedom Bowl in Anaheim Stadium.

"Names and logos don't mean anything," a defensive Smith commented after the game. He said it was only the members of the media who were shocked by the outcome, because they didn't understand college football. "You don't beat someone just because of your name and logo."

Whatever the merits of the argument, the embattled Smith further alienated the Trojan faithful with his comments. But even before Smith reached the locker room, the look on athletic director Mike McGee's ashen face told the story: Smith would not be back as the Trojans' coach for 1993.

Instead, John Robinson, who had much success as the Los Angeles Rams head coach after leaving USC following the 1982 season, returned to resuscitate the program. For a while it worked. Robinson led the Trojans to three successive bowl wins, including two New Year's Day bowls.

The first, actually on January 2, came in the Cotton Bowl to cap the 1994 season. USC stunned the partisan Texas Tech crowd with a 28-point first quarter and won in a rout 55–14. Wide receiver Keyshawn Johnson caught 3 scoring passes and amassed 222 yards on 7 receptions for the Trojans, but he was just warming up. The next year, Johnson caught 12 passes—all of them for first downs—for 216 yards in a 41–32 victory over third-ranked Northwestern.

The Cinderella Wildcats had been the darlings of the nation en route to their first Rose Bowl in half a century, and Robinson didn't like the way his team had been left out of the spotlight.

"Most of us have bruises on our toes from the way you people [the media] shoved us out of the way," he said. And: "Our toes were more than stepped on. They were trampled."

While what Robinson said was true, it was a strangely undignified display from a coach who always had exuded class in victory or defeat. Moreover, the chip didn't seem to leave his shoulder, and he struggled through 6–6 and 6–5 seasons in 1996 and 1997 while reportedly feuding with athletic director Mike Garrett.

Robinson was not asked back for the 1998 season. Instead, former Robinson assistant Paul Hackett, a successful offensive coordinator in the pros but a flop at Pittsburgh in his lone stint as a college head coach, was brought in. Hackett quickly accomplished something no USC coach had done since 1951: He won

USC Coaching Records (since 1960)

	W	L	T	Pct
John McKay (1960–75)	127	40	8	.749
John Robinson (1976–82, 1993–97)	104	35	4	.741
Ted Tollner (1983–86)	26	20	1	.564
Larry Smith (1987–92)	44	25	3	.632
Paul Hackett (1998–2000)	19	18	0	.514
Pete Carroll (2001–04)	42	9	0	.824

his first game. While trailing Purdue 17–10 in the 1998 opener at the Coliseum, the new coach turned to heralded freshman Carson Palmer to direct key drives to a touchdown and a field goal, and the Trojans went on to win 27–17.

Unfortunately that may have been the high point of Hackett's tenure. Players had trouble with his supersized, NFL-style playbook, and he struggled with issues such as clock management. Hackett's last USC team, in 2000, was characterized by the most undisciplined play—poor tackling, untimely penalties, turnovers, and unsportsmanlike conduct—that most Trojan fans had seen in their lifetimes.

Hackett was fired after having compiled a three-year record of just 19–18. His dismissal had a big silver lining, though: Pete Carroll soon was hired to return USC football to national prominence.

The Best Ever?

After the Trojans pounded Arkansas 31–10 in the 1972 season opener, strong-armed Razorbacks quarterback Joe Ferguson sat wearily in the locker room. "If USC doesn't go undefeated," he sighed, "something is wrong."

Turned out, nothing was wrong. In fact just about everything was right for the Trojans in 1972, when they cruised to the national championship with a 12–0 record. Moreover, head coach John McKay built one of the most dominant teams in the history of college football that season.

"It was the best, most physical all-around team we've ever had," said the late Marv Goux, a USC assistant coach and the Trojans' inspirational leader. Goux believed that the groundwork for the outstanding 1972 season was laid in the spring that year. "We had decent teams the previous two years [USC was 6–4–1 both seasons], but the coaches knew we were better than that," he said. "We had gotten kind of complacent, and our guys didn't realize what it took."

So instead of the usual spring drills, McKay took the Trojans across the street to the Coliseum, where they scrimmaged over and over. "It was big man on big man, day after day," Goux said. "Coach McKay said that by the time we're through we're either going to be dead or we're going to be a good football team." It turned out to be a great football team.

Senior Mike Rae was the starting quarterback and often was relieved by, as he says, "some little blond kid playing behind me. I don't recall his name." (It was sophomore Pat Haden.) They threw to pass catchers such as flanker Lynn Swann and tight end Charles Young, plus split ends Edesel Garrison and Johnny McKay, the coach's son. Rod McNeill was the starter among a bevy of tailbacks, but he eventually gave way to sophomore sensation Anthony Davis. All-America fullback Sam "Bam" Cunningham and All-America tackle Pete Adams led the blocking. On defense, tackle John Grant and linebacker Richard "Batman" Wood were the headline grabbers.

USC entered the season ranked eighth in the nation—but still not without question marks. Indeed, the two previous Trojan squads also began the season ranked among the nation's top ten

That's a portrait of
Howard Jones over-
looking John McKay
at work. AP

before stumbling. Plus, Troy returned only four starters on defense and faced a tough schedule that began on the road at fourth-ranked Arkansas, a team with national championship aspirations of its own.

But after its rout of the Razorbacks, USC ascended all the way to number one, and the Trojans stayed there the rest of the season. They outscored their opponents 467–134. They never trailed in the second half of any game. And when it was all over, they became the first team in college football history to be penciled in as number one on every ballot in both the writers' and coaches' polls.

USC's 1972 team not only was its most talented ever, but McKay also said it was his closest team ever. That group shared a common goal to become one of the greatest squads of all time.

"We felt something special," says Wood, who earned All-America honors for the first of three successive seasons that year. "We had so much talent at every position, and we were trying to show that we were the best. We thought we could play with anybody, even the professional teams."

Longtime television broadcaster Keith Jackson still calls the 1972 Trojans the greatest college football team he's ever seen. So, too, does Wood. "We proved we were the best," he said. In fact, it's hard to find a dissenting opinion outside of, say, Norman, Oklahoma, or South Bend, Indiana, or Lincoln, Nebraska.

One man who demurred, though (sort of), was Washington State head coach Jim Sweeney. USC blasted the Cougars 44–3 for win number nine that season, and Sweeney shook McKay's hand at midfield after the game. "John," Sweeney said, "you're not the number-one team in the country. The Miami Dolphins are better."

Here's how USC forged its perfect season in 1972:

USC 31, Arkansas 10 (1–0)

Fullback Manfred Moore fumbled the opening kickoff, and the Razorbacks recovered. It was not an auspicious beginning for the Trojans—but it pretty much turned out to be the low point of the season. "It was planned," McKay deadpanned at his weekly meeting with reporters several days later. "We wanted to test our defense early."

The defense held, limiting Arkansas to a field goal, and the offense took over after that. Mike Rae was named the conference player of the week after completing 18 of 24 passes for 269 yards. He ran 5 yards for a touchdown, set up 3 other touchdowns with long pass completions, and kicked a field goal.

McKay refused to speculate about the prospects of a national championship. "How will we do the rest of the season?" he countered a reporter's question. "The worst we can be is 1–10."

USC 51, Oregon State 6 (2–0)

McKay had been worried about his defense before the start of the season. If the opener didn't alleviate his concerns, this game sure did. USC held the Beavers to only 92 yards while winning in a rout.

The offense did its part, also, with Rae passing for 248 yards on only 12 completions and McNeill rushing for 111 yards and 3 touchdowns. The Trojans amassed 670 yards in all, with 99 of them coming on a touchdown drive in the third quarter.

USC 55, Illinois 20 (3–0)

The Trojans led just 20–14 at halftime, and McKay was furious. "This is ridiculous," he told his players. The outmanned Illini had led twice, by scores of 7–0 and 14–7. It was a measure of

McKay's First Championship Team

"We knew we were going to be a pretty good football team in 1962," assistant coach Marv Goux said thirty years later. But the Trojans didn't know how good.

"That's because the staff basically had us brainwashed to concentrate only on our first game against Duke," said Damon Bame, a guard and linebacker for Troy that year. "John McKay didn't want any of us thinking about national championships or the conference season or anything else."

USC was unranked when it opened its 1962 season at the Coliseum against the number-eight Blue Devils. The Trojans won 14–7 and immediately vaulted to ninth in the rankings. Their defense opened some eyes that day, also. "It was an Arkansas variation on the old Oklahoma five-two," said Bame, the signal caller for USC's 1962 defense.

McKay, an offensive innovator who was introducing his version of the I-formation to college football, also had tweaked Frank Broyles's Arkansas defense. The result in 1962 was a dominating unit that permitted ten regular-season opponents only 55 points. Eight teams failed to score more than 7 points. "We were not a big team," Goux said. "We had a lot of small guys, but everybody did their part."

The Trojans became number one after beating Navy 13–6 in game eight. Then they clinched the national title with wins over UCLA (14–3) and Notre Dame (25–0) before downing number-two Wisconsin in the Rose Bowl (42–37 in a game that was 42–14 in the fourth quarter).

Here's a capsule look at each of USC's eleven national championship teams:

1928: Howard Jones's Thundering Herd won its first national title by going 9-0-1. The Trojans capped the season with a 27-14 victory over Notre Dame, but the key win was a 10-0 shutout of Pop Warner's powerful Stanford team.

1931: The Trojans were stunned by St. Mary's 13-7 in the opener but then reeled off ten consecutive victories while outscoring their opponents 356-39. The signature victory was a monumental 16-14 upset of Notre Dame in South Bend.

1932: Another of college football's greatest teams, the 1932 Trojans were hardly tested while posting a 10-0 record. USC shut out eight opponents and allowed only 13 points all season.

1939: Only a pair of ties blemished the Trojans' ten-game schedule in 1939. USC capped the season with a 14-0 shutout of Tennessee in the Rose Bowl on New Year's Day 1940, snapping the Volunteers' twenty-three-game winning streak.

1962: Defense was the name of the game for the 1962 Trojans. But John McKay also had a talented offense that featured quarterbacks Pete Beathard and Bill Nelsen and end Hal Bedsole.

1967: USC avenged a humiliating shutout to Notre Dame to close the 1966 regular season by beating the fifth-ranked Irish 24-7 for the Trojans' first win in South Bend since 1939. That—and O.J.'s run against UCLA—led to a national title.

1972: USC compiled its 12-0 record against a slate of heavyweights. Half of its opponents were ranked in the top twenty before Troy beat them, with three rated among the top ten.

(continued)

1974: After the dramatic comebacks over Notre Dame (55–24) and Ohio State (18–17) to end the season, USC got a gift from an unlikely source: Ara Parseghian. In his last game the Irish coach engineered an upset of Alabama in the Orange Bowl on New Year's night, paving the way for the Trojans to become number one in the final UPI poll.

1978: USC went 12–1 and beat then-number-one Alabama 24–14 in Birmingham early in the season. Still, the Crimson Tide was awarded Associated Press's half of the national championship; the Trojans took UPI's.

2003: Troy won its first national championship in twenty-five years behind a blistering offense that amassed 534 points in a 12–1 season. The top-ranked Trojans beat number-four Michigan 28–14 to clinch Associated Press's version of the national title.

2004: Spurned by the Bowl Championship Series's complicated formula for matching teams in its championship game the year before, the Trojans set out to claim both halves of the national title—and they did. USC went wire-to-wire atop the polls, then blasted Oklahoma 55–19 in the Orange Bowl for its thirteenth win without a loss.

USC's dominance in 1972 that it was one of only three games in which Troy would trail at any point.

McKay's players got the message loud and clear. Backup tailback Anthony Davis capped a 64-yard drive to open the third quarter with a 2-yard touchdown run, and the Trojans went on to score 35 points in the second half, turning the game into a rout.

Actually, the key play of the game came late in the first half. With the score tied 14–14 and Illinois on the move, reserve linebacker Ed Powell sacked quarterback Tom McCartney for a big loss, forced a fumble, and recovered the ball. USC scored on every possession after that except when it ran out the clock at the end of the game.

Davis scored two times, while Rae and Johnny McKay teamed on a pair of touchdown passes. Still, the elder McKay was not satisfied. "We didn't play very well," he groused afterward. Tell that to the Illini.

USC 51, Michigan State 6 (4–0)

After the offensive explosion against Illinois, it was the defense's turn against Michigan State. Sure, the Trojans surpassed 50 points for the third consecutive game, but most of it was set up on the defensive side of the ball, where USC throttled the Spartans' Wishbone attack.

The Trojans recovered 5 fumbles and intercepted 3 passes, which they converted into 6 touchdowns. Richard Wood returned an interception for a touchdown, and USC scored 28 fourth-quarter points on scoring drives of zero (Wood's touchdown), one, two, and five offensive plays.

Special teams got into the act, also. Lynn Swann returned a punt 92 yards for a touchdown and set up a field goal with a 28-yard runback.

USC 30, Stanford 21 (5–0)

USC trailed 10–7 early in this one. It would be the last time all season that the Trojans were behind in any game. Troy erased its deficit before halftime when the Cardinal made a couple of critical mistakes on special teams. USC scored a touchdown after recovering a muffed punt, then added another after a poor punt snap led to good field position.

Though the game is generally regarded as one of the few times the 1972 team faced much of a challenge, the Trojans still pretty much had their way with the Cardinal. USC amassed 407 total yards to just 183 for Stanford. And the score was 30–13 before the Cardinal scored a late touchdown.

Northern and Southern Californians have never been particularly enamored of each other in any venue, and the rivalry extended to Stanford and USC. Frustration at the treatment his players had received for years in Palo Alto boiled over for an angry McKay, who said afterward that he'd beat Stanford by "2,000 points if I could." Cardinal coach John Ralston was no more gracious, calling McKay a skunk, and his players followed suit. "I don't think they're all that good," one Stanford player said. "SC ain't [bleep]," said another. Only he didn't say "bleep."

USC 42, California 14 (6–0)

Reeling from the criticism he received for his comments after the Stanford game, McKay was relatively quiet after an easy victory over the Trojans' other Bay Area rivals. "I'm always subdued," McKay protested. "I was subdued for twelve years, and the one time I wasn't I get called a vindictive old man."

USC afforded McKay an opportunity to relax with an easy win. It was 21–0 at halftime, and the Trojans never looked back.

Rae and Cunningham each rushed for 2 touchdowns. Pat Haden, Rae's backup, completed only 3 of 11 passes, but two of his connections went for scores to Charles Young.

USC 34, Washington 7 (7-0)

This was the day that Anthony Davis officially arrived as the next great Trojan tailback. The sophomore came off the bench to rush for 91 yards and 2 touchdowns, including a spectacular 14-yard run on which he lined up at flanker and bowled over various defenders on his way to the goal line. Davis's performance earned him a spot in the starting lineup the rest of the season.

A good team with an excellent defense, Washington was one of the favorites (along with USC) to win the Pac-8 crown in 1972. But the Huskies put up little fight while hampered by key injuries, especially at quarterback.

The Trojans raced to a 20–0 lead at intermission and built the advantage to 34–0 through three quarters. By the end USC had outgained the Huskies 406 yards to 120. In twenty-two attempts, Washington quarterbacks completed almost as many passes to Trojan defenders (5) as they did to Husky receivers (7).

The primary victim of a ferocious USC pass defense was eighteen-year-old quarterback Denny Fitzpatrick, who saw his first collegiate action in this game. "SC sure can hit, can't they?" he said afterward.

USC 18, Oregon 0 (8-0)

On a wet and rainy afternoon in Eugene, the Trojans and Ducks were mired in a scoreless tie until Davis took charge.

After USC took possession at midfield in the third quarter, Davis, making his first career start, burst 48 yards on a sweep for the game's first score. Then the Trojans forced a punt and took over on their own 45 yard line. Davis took the ball on another sweep and burst around end for 55 yards and another touchdown.

Two plays, 103 yards. Davis would go on to carry the ball 25 times for 206 yards. USC's defense did the rest, keeping the Ducks and their star quarterback, Dan Fouts, off the board. Richard Wood's interception led to a fourth-quarter touchdown run by Cunningham that sealed the outcome.

USC 44, Washington State 3 (9–0)

Back in the Pacific Northwest for the second successive week, the Trojans rolled over the Cougars by keeping the ball on the ground. USC piled up 349 yards and 5 touchdowns rushing. Davis did most of the damage, accounting for 195 yards on 31 carries and scoring three times.

Ed Powell returned an interception for a touchdown, and the Trojans converted five Washington State turnovers into 21 points. A short punt led to another touchdown. With the victory, USC improved to 6–0 in conference play and set up a Rose Bowl showdown with UCLA two weeks later.

USC 24, UCLA 7 (10–0)

The Bruins had opened the season by beating number-one Nebraska (paving the way for USC to move into the top spot), but they never had a chance to topple number one in this game. Davis had more than 100 yards by halftime and finished with 178 yards. He had a 23-yard touchdown run, while McNeill and Rae (who passed only twelve times) also rushed for scores.

The Trojans already had shut down one Wishbone attack in Michigan State earlier in the year. And while fourteenth-ranked

USC's Statistical Leaders in 1972

RUSHING	No.	Yds.	Avg.	TD	
Anthony Davis	207	1,191	5.8	17	

PASSING	Att.	Comp.	Yds.	TD	Int.
Mike Rae	199	114	1,754	5	12

RECEIVING	No.	Yds.	Avg.	TD
Charles Young	29	470	16.2	3

SCORING	TD	PAT	FG	Pts.
Anthony Davis	19	0	0	114

PUNTING	No.	Yds.	Avg.
Dave Boulware	49	1,761	36.1

INTERCEPTIONS	No.	Yds.	Avg.	TD
Artimus Parker	6	107	17.8	0

KICKOFF RETURNS	No.	Yds.	Avg.	TD
Anthony Davis	12	468	39.0	2

PUNT RETURNS	No.	Yds.	Avg.	TD
Lynn Swann	19	253	13.3	1

TACKLES	No.
Richard Wood	129

UCLA got its share of yards on the ground (198), they mostly came between the 20 yard lines. Wood made 18 tackles to help USC secure a Rose Bowl berth.

The Best of the Rest

USC's 1979 team may have been the best in college football history *not* to win a national championship.

The Trojans featured Heisman Trophy–winning tailback Charles White running behind a stellar offensive line that included future NFL stars such as Brad Budde, Roy Foster, and Keith Van Horne. Future Heisman winner Marcus Allen was primarily a blocking back. Quarterback Paul McDonald and wide receiver Kevin Williams formed a prolific touchdown-producing combo through the air. Tight end Hoby Brenner could block or catch passes equally well.

On defense, linebackers Riki Gray, Dennis Johnson, and Larry McGrew were stars; defensive backs Ronnie Lott and Dennis Smith helped give USC one of the best secondaries in college football; and other players such as freshman nose guard George Achica and sophomore linebacker Chip Banks were just beginning to come into their own. In all, twelve players from that team went on to become first-round NFL draft choices. Dozens more went on to play in the pros, not only in the NFL, but also in the United States Football League.

With such a wealth of talent and coming off a 12–1 season in which they won a share of the national championship, the Trojans predictably were ranked number one to start the season. They maintained that standing with several easy wins and one close one—a come-from-behind effort at LSU in which McDonald tossed the winning touchdown pass to Williams with 32 seconds left—before stumbling against Stanford.

On Homecoming Day, USC raced to a 21–0 halftime lead. But the Cardinal roared back to forge a 21–21 tie. Diminutive Stanford running back Mike Dotterer knotted the score with 4:30 remaining on a short touchdown run in which he zigged and zagged around several Trojan defenders who tried to bring him down. Both teams had a chance to win with field goal tries after that, but the game ended deadlocked.

After tying Stanford, USC fell to number four in the rankings. Troy didn't lose again, winning its last six games, including routs of Notre Dame (42–23) and UCLA (49–14). And, although it was too late for their national title hopes, the Trojans achieved a measure of redemption by driving the length of the field for a touchdown in the closing moments against Ohio State in the Rose Bowl. USC's 17–16 victory over the top-ranked Buckeyes denied Woody Hayes's team the national title, and USC finished second to unbeaten Alabama.

Anthony Davis enjoys the morning paper after the Notre Dame game in 1972.
Wally Fong/AP

USC 45, Notre Dame 23 (11–0)

Anthony Davis, who made a career out of tormenting Notre Dame, erupted for 6 touchdowns—4 rushing and 2 on kick returns—as USC completed a perfect regular season.

It wasn't as easy as the final score indicated, though. The tenth-ranked Irish controlled possession for much of the game and actually outgained the Trojans for the afternoon. And late in the third quarter, Tom Clements's third touchdown pass of the game pulled Notre Dame within 2 points at 25–23. But the Irish missed a two-point conversion try, and then Davis dashed their upset hopes by returning the ensuing kickoff 96 yards for a touchdown. Davis, who also returned the game's opening kickoff 97 yards for a score, added rushing touchdowns of 1, 5, 4, and 8 yards.

By winning, the Trojans wrapped up UPI's version of the national championship. The Associated Press did not name its winner until after the bowl games.

USC 42, Ohio State 17 (12-0)

In the weeks leading up to the game, Ohio State coach Woody Hayes lobbied for votes as the Associated Press national champion in the event his third-ranked Buckeyes upset the favored Trojans. He needn't have bothered.

The game was tied 7–7 at halftime, but the Trojans blew it open by reaching the end zone on each of their first five possessions of the second half. Rae passed for 229 yards, and Davis rushed for 157 yards, but most of the scoring was done by Cunningham, who rushed for a Rose Bowl–record 4 touchdowns. All of his scores came on short touchdown dives over the top of the pile at the goal line.

Afterwards, the cantankerous Hayes met with reporters only briefly and after a long delay. But even he had to admit that the 1972 Trojans were the best college team he'd ever seen. Meanwhile, in the other locker room, a bemused John McKay asked, "Is there anybody else the Associated Press would like us to play?"

55-24!

In November of 1974, with his team being pounded 24–0 by its biggest rival just before halftime in front of 83,000 fans in its home stadium and millions more watching on national television, USC head coach John McKay never saw what was coming: an epic rally that lifted the Trojans to a 55–24 victory for the greatest chapter in the history of the greatest intersectional rivalry in college football.

USC's come-from-behind victory over the Irish in 1964 gave John McKay a lift. AP

McKay's first thought, in fact, was of 1966. That was the year Notre Dame humiliated USC 51–0. Irish head coach Ara Parseghian, two months removed from a 17–17 tie with Michigan State in which his conservative play calling brought stinging criticism, poured it on. He handed USC the worst defeat in school history while impressing the voters enough to wrap up the national title. "If he can, he'll beat us 51–0 again," McKay grumbled to assistant coach Dave Levy at his side that day in 1974.

But Craig Fertig was thinking about a different USC–Notre Dame game. Fertig, who watched the 1974 game from the sidelines, was the Trojans quarterback when they played the Irish in 1964. In that game, top-ranked and unbeaten Notre Dame bolted to a 17–0 halftime lead before USC rallied for a 20–17 upset.

That was one of the signature games in the USC–Notre Dame series—though it soon would pale in comparison to what was about to unfold in the next couple of hours at the Los Ange-

Trojan Horse

The headline in the next day's *Los Angeles Times* said it all: "Davis! Davis! Davis! Davis! Davis! Davis!" USC tailback Anthony Davis scored a school-record 6 touchdowns to lead the top-ranked Trojans to a 45–23 rout of number-ten Notre Dame at the Coliseum in 1972.

Davis returned the game's opening kickoff 97 yards for a touchdown, and the Trojans never looked back while improving to 11–0 and to the brink of the national championship (which they secured several weeks later by beating Ohio State in the Rose Bowl). He returned another kickoff 96 yards for a touchdown, and added scoring runs of 1, 5, 4, and 8 yards.

Still, Davis is best known for his 4-touchdown effort against the Irish in 1974, when USC erased a 24–0 deficit to win 55–24. His touchdown return of the second half kickoff ignited the Trojans' 35-point third quarter.

"The funny thing is that people mix up the 1972 and 1974 games," says author Jim Perry, who was USC's sports information director at the time. "Davis had big games in both, both were played in the Coliseum, and in both he had touchdown returns down the same sideline."

The games certainly are a blur to Irish fans, who witnessed Davis score a remarkable 11 touchdowns against them in his three years, including one in Notre Dame's 23–14 win in 1973.

Davis was one of the best USC tailbacks *not* to win the Heisman Trophy. He led the Trojans in rushing three consecutive seasons, topped by 1,421 yards as a senior in 1974, when he was a unanimous All-America selection. He also completed his eligibility holding numerous school and NCAA records for kickoff returns.

But Davis had the misfortune of having a big senior year at the same time that Ohio State running back Archie Griffin emerged as a national star. Davis was the runner-up in the 1974 Heisman balloting to Griffin, who won again in 1975 and is still the only player to earn the award twice.

les Memorial Coliseum. Because neither McKay nor Fertig nor any of the other participants and spectators could have foreseen the dizzying sequence of events that ensued.

It was not only the reversal of fortune that made the Trojans' 55–24 win so dramatic. It also was the set of circumstances surrounding the game: USC was ranked sixth in the country, the Irish fifth. Notre Dame entered the game with the nation's top-ranked defense and had allowed only 9 touchdowns in their first ten games. In just seventeen minutes of playing time, the Trojans erupted for 8 scores.

As split end Johnny McKay, the coach's son, marveled in the locker room afterward, "Against Notre Dame? Maybe against Kent State—but Notre Dame?"

The genesis of the comeback came in the closing seconds of the first half, when USC tailback Anthony Davis took a short pass from quarterback Pat Haden and raced 7 yards for a touchdown to make the score 24–6. Though the extra point was blocked, the Trojans suddenly had a glimmer of hope.

"The biggest thing is that we scored right before the end of the first half," Johnny McKay said. "They had dominated the game up to then."

At intermission the elder McKay, rescued from his malaise by Davis's touchdown, invoked the memory of USC's come-from-behind win ten years earlier and emphasized the importance of scoring on the opening possession of the third quarter.

The Trojans did that in only 14 seconds—the amount of time that it took Davis to race 102 yards down the left sideline with the second-half kickoff. Suddenly, the normally complacent Coliseum crowd was rocking.

The USC–Notre Dame series is the greatest intersectional rivalry in college football.
Joe Robbins

A failed two-point conversion try left USC trailing still by 12 points, but the floodgates were open. Davis ran 6 yards for a touchdown to cap a short drive the next time the Trojans had the ball, and he gave USC the lead for the first time midway through the third quarter by running 4 yards for another score after the Trojans recovered an Irish fumble.

Then, in rapid succession, Haden tossed touchdown passes of 18 and 45 yards to McKay and 16 yards to Shelton Diggs. Charles Phillips's 58-yard interception return early in the fourth period ended the 55-point outburst and left the Irish shell-shocked.

"There's never been such a turn of momentum in any other game I've been involved with," Haden said ten years later. "It just snowballed."

5 5 - 2 4 !   83

Win One for the Fat Guy

Only days before the USC–Notre Dame game in 1982, head coach John Robinson revealed that he was resigning after seven seasons at the helm in order to take a position with the school's administration. While announcing the move—and simultaneously poking fun at his ample girth—he urged his team to "win one for the fat guy" in the final game of his first tour of duty with the Trojans, who were not eligible to play in a bowl that year.

It wasn't exactly an impassioned plea, such as Fighting Irish coach Knute Rockne's exhortation to his troops to "win one for the Gipper" before Notre Dame's game against Army in 1928. For that matter, it wasn't exactly a plea. "I was just trying to make light of the fact that I was leaving," Robinson said.

Trojan players and fans, however, mindful of the school's remarkable run under Robinson—four bowl wins, a national championship, and three top-five finishes in the polls—took the message to heart. They wanted to send Robinson out with a win, and they did—but barely. USC trailed Notre Dame 13–10 late in the game, when tailback Michael Harper capped a lengthy drive in the fourth quarter by diving over the goal line from 1 yard out for the winning touchdown with 48 seconds to play.

Trojans linebacker Richard Wood had no explanation for the turnaround. "I was in the middle of it, and I can't explain it," he said. "Everything we did worked, and everything they did turned into disaster. It was like a wild dream, like we weren't in control."

The victory helped propel USC to the national championship five weeks later, when the Trojans edged number-three Ohio State 18–17 in the Rose Bowl.

Or did he? Irish players and coaches howled that Harper lost the ball before he crossed the goal line. A Notre Dame player, in fact, cradled the ball in the end zone. But the officials huddled, then ruled that the touchdown stood. The Trojans won 17–13.

In defense of the officials, nobody saw the ball come loose. I had left my press box seat midway through the fourth quarter and watched the decisive play on the sidelines at the goal line—virtually the same view that the line judge had. I never saw a fumble, though a Notre Dame supporter standing next to me was beside himself after seeing an Irish player frantically waving the ball in the face of an official.

After the game, I was sent into the officials' locker room to obtain a pool quote from the referee. He explained that Harper had crossed the goal line for a touchdown before losing the ball on the "throwback"—that is, when the defense pushed him back after stopping his forward momentum. The referee had me read his quote back to him before releasing it to the assembled media, and I was glad he did. As several reporters were quick to point out in the newspapers the next day, there was no throwback on the play.

Notre Dame players and fans vowed revenge for the perceived injustice, and they got it. USC did not beat the Irish again until 1996.

The dramatic win against the Irish also quickly became one of the most memorable college football games ever. A quarter of a century later, as the year 2000 approached, the game was ranked sixth on both the *Sport Magazine* and *Football News* top college football moments of the twentieth century.

It is the classic game in a classic series. Unlike many other great rivalries, the USC–Notre Dame series is not characterized by hatred but by mutual respect. Nor was it borne out of a provincial desire to establish territory or through conference association. Instead, the series is noteworthy because it has consistently produced great players making great plays in great games.

It is Joe Montana and the underdog Irish coming out of the locker room in green jerseys, stirring Notre Dame fans into a frenzy before Notre Dame's 49–19 rout in 1977; Frank Jordan racing onto the field to kick the game-winning field goal for USC as time ran out the following year; Jabari Holloway pouncing on a fumble for the winning touchdown in Notre Dame's come-from-behind, 25–24 victory in 1999; and freshman Reggie Bush sprinting 58 yards untouched for a touchdown in the Trojans' rout in 2003.

It is a series filled with Heisman Trophy winners (thirteen of them) and national champions (twenty-one between the two schools). And it is a series that almost always holds national significance. Fifty-eight times in the sixty-six meetings since rankings have been kept, either USC or Notre Dame has been in the polls at the time of its annual game. Both teams have been ranked twenty-nine times. And both teams have been ranked among the top ten in the nation fifteen times. The Trojans have spoiled Notre Dame's perfect seasons five times in the rivalry game; Notre Dame has returned the favor on six occasions.

For the late Marv Goux, like for many others, nothing can match the USC–Notre Dame series. He was on the Trojans sidelines for twenty-nine games against the Irish, and his enthusiasm for the series never waned.

"It was always *the* game for me," he said. "There's just something about it. When I recruited kids, I would tell them that by going to USC, they would most likely play in a Rose Bowl—

maybe even two or three—and they could quite possibly win a national championship. But the one thing they'd enjoy more than anything else was playing against Notre Dame."

Goux enjoyed the experience three times as a center and linebacker in the 1950s. He made Notre Dame's All-Opponents teams in both 1954 and 1955 (the Trojans pummeled fifth-ranked Notre Dame 42–20 in the latter game). "Of all the awards and honors I've ever received," he once said, "they mean the most to me. If my house was burning down, those are the ones I'd go in and grab."

That there is a USC–Notre Dame series at all is thanks in large part to Bonnie Skiles Rockne, the wife of legendary Irish coach Knute Rockne. Knute was a college football coach, but he was a husband first. So even as Rockne was politely declining USC graduate manager Gwynn Wilson's offer of a home-and-home series with the Irish while on the observation car of a train headed from Nebraska to Indiana in November of 1925, Bonnie was plotting with Wilson's wife to escape the rigors of the bitter Midwestern winter with a trip to California every other year.

Actually, Bonnie long had been sold on sunny California and was hopeful of making the move west when USC approached her husband about its vacant head coaching position earlier in the year. But Notre Dame persuaded Rockne to stay in South Bend, and the Trojans job went to Howard Jones instead.

Jones wanted to build USC's program from a strong regional power to a national contender, and he wanted a series that would attract attention around the country. Everyone knew Notre Dame, so he sent Wilson and his new bride to Nebraska—where the Fighting Irish were playing the Cornhuskers in the final year of an agreement between the schools—to talk to Rockne.

"He told me that he couldn't meet with USC because Notre Dame already was traveling too much," Wilson said many years later. "The team had gotten the nickname the 'Ramblers,' which he didn't like."

Once Knute and Bonnie were alone, however, the Irish coach changed his mind—or she changed it for him. Knute went back to find Wilson on the train and told him that he'd reconsidered. The series began one year later.

Almost immediately, the intersectional produced thrills. In the first game, the Irish escaped with a 1-point victory when diminutive backup quarterback Art Parisien came off the bench in the fourth quarter and passed for the winning touchdown with two minutes left.

Notre Dame won again by a single point the next year, though the real story was at the turnstiles. More than 120,000 fans packed Chicago's Soldier Field to witness the Irish's 7–6 triumph.

USC's first win came at the Coliseum in 1928, but it was in 1931 that the series first produced a classic game that really put it on the national map. Notre Dame, which entered the game in South Bend riding a twenty-six-game unbeaten string and apparently en route to a national title, took a 14–0 lead into the fourth quarter. But the Trojans rallied for 16 points in the final period, the last 3 coming on Johnny Baker's 33-yard field goal with one minute left, to win 16–14. When the Trojans returned home, more than 300,000 fans greeted them with a ticker-tape parade through downtown Los Angeles.

USC's comeback in the 1964 Notre Dame game was equally remarkable. After spotting the Irish 17 points in the first half, the Trojans chipped away, pulling within 17–13 in the fourth quarter.

The Shillelagh

Any tourist stop in Ireland can sell you a memento called a *shillelagh,* but such trinkets are a far cry from the genuine article. The original shillelagh was a Gaelic war club; later, Irishmen carried shillelaghs as a defense against muggers and thieves. Its hard wood, usually blackthorn, is accentuated by a root knob at the end that makes it a fearsome weapon.

It is such a shillelagh, handcrafted in Ireland, that is presented annually to the winner of the USC–Notre Dame game. The winning school keeps possession of the trophy for the year and adds a medallion in the shape of a Trojan head or an Irish shamrock.

In 1988 the shillelagh was shipped to USC for a photo shoot celebrating the school's athletic centennial. Perhaps a metaphor for the decrepit state of the rivalry—which had suffered during the lean tenures of head coaches Ted Tollner at USC and Gerry Faust at Notre Dame—the trophy was in disrepair, with old medallions falling off and little space for new ones.

When the schools played that November, however, Notre Dame was number one in the polls, and USC was number two—the first time since 1980 that both schools were ranked going into the game. Quarterback Tony Rice's spectacular running helped lift the Irish to a 27–10 victory that year and helped restore national luster to the rivalry.

The original shillelagh was restored, also, and eventually was retired and put on permanent display at Notre Dame. A new shillelagh commemorates the series winners since 1990.

Mike Williams makes a key touchdown catch in the 2002 game.
Mark J. Terrill/AP

With 1:33 to play, USC faced fourth-and-8 from Notre Dame's 15 yard line. Flanker Rod Sherman suggested a play to McKay, and the coach obliged. Sherman beat his man to the goal line, and Fertig's pass led him perfectly for the winning touchdown. "I remember crossing the goal line in the closed end of the Coliseum, and I couldn't believe the amount of noise," Sherman said twenty years later.

Overall, Notre Dame leads the series 42–29–5, though in recent years the tide has turned in USC's favor. In 1997 the Trojans ended a thirteen-game winless streak with a stunning 27–20 victory in overtime. A missed extra point opened the door for USC to tie the game late in the fourth quarter.

The win merely salvaged a 6–6 season for the Trojans, but it was literally a costly defeat for the Irish, who fell to 10–2 and out of a major revenue Bowl Championship Series berth. "Right now my guts just feel like someone reached in and cut out my insides," Irish head coach Lou Holtz lamented afterward. "I've never felt this low."

It turned out to be Holtz's last game for the school. Notre Dame refused a lesser bowl bid, and Holtz resigned soon afterward.

Two years later, unranked USC dealt the ninth-rated Irish their first shutout loss in eleven years, winning 10–0 at the Coliseum. And in 2002, 2003, and 2004, the Trojans pummeled Notre Dame, winning 44–13 in Los Angeles, then 45–14 in South Bend, and 41–10 in L.A. again. USC amassed 610 total yards—the most ever by an Irish opponent—in the 2002 game. Carson Palmer's 425 passing yards that evening set another Notre Dame opponents' record and swayed enough voters to help make him the Trojans' fifth Heisman Trophy winner. Matt Leinart's 400 yards and 5 touchdown passes in the 2004 game paved the way for USC's sixth Heisman.

For All the Marbles

USC trailed UCLA 20–14 early in the fourth quarter of a monumental rivalry game at the Los Angeles Coliseum in 1967 when Trojans quarterback Toby Page approached the line of scrimmage on third down from the Trojans' 36 yard line. Page saw the Bruins linebackers drop back, expecting a pass. "Red!" he hollered. An audible. "Red 23!" As in 23

USC's Pat Cashman picks off a pass in the 1967 game against UCLA. AP

Blast, a conventional USC running play designed to gain 4, maybe 5, yards. "Oh, no," thought Trojans tailback O. J. Simpson. "That's a horrible call."

And with 8 yards to go for a first down, a 5-yard play may not have looked like the most inspired decision to the 90,772 fans in attendance or to the national television audience. But Simpson quickly got those 5 yards and a lot more. He took the handoff and burst through the left side of the line. At the Bruins' 40, he cut back toward the middle of the field and was off to the races.

Though O.J. already was exhausted from having carried the ball repeatedly for three quarters (he would finish the game with

30 carries for 177 yards), he easily pulled away from the pursuit to complete a 64-yard touchdown run. It lifted USC to a 21–20 victory over the Bruins and arguably is the greatest single play in the Trojans' long and storied football history.

It certainly is the most memorable play in the history of the USC-UCLA rivalry, a series that began modestly in 1929 — modestly because the Trojans' 76–0 rout that year and their 52–0 romp the next year were so one-sided that the series was put on hold for several seasons until the Bruins became more competitive.

That's not a put-down; it's just that the school was only a few years removed from a small downtown campus that identified itself as the Southern Branch of the University of California system. To this day, if you really want to get the goat of a UCLA fan, "Southern Branch" is a good place to start.

Once the series resumed in 1936, the Bruins immediately posed a greater challenge, forging ties of 7–7 that season, 0–0 in 1939, and 7–7 in 1941 before finally winning 14–7 in 1942, the ninth meeting between the schools. With wartime travel restrictions in place from 1943 to 1945, USC and UCLA played each other twice each season; since then they've met once each year.

"The game is not life or death," the late, great Bruins head coach Red Sanders was fond of saying. "It's more important than that." It's more important because of the location of the two schools. It's only about 14 miles west on the Santa Monica Freeway and north on the San Diego Freeway to go door-to-door from USC to UCLA. Such geographical proximity has bred an animosity like no other college football rivalry.

It's somewhat rare that two major universities are so close to one another. It's rarer still that such schools have two of the nation's most formidable athletic programs. That means that anytime USC and UCLA meet—in any sport, but especially in football—Los Angeles residents choose up sides. Husbands from USC are at odds with their wives from UCLA, coworkers with Trojan allegiances square off against those with Bruin ties. And for the loser, it's a long, long year until the schools meet again.

"If you don't win this game," the late USC assistant coach Marv Goux used to say, "you can't go to the beach, you can't go to the movies, you can't go anywhere."

More often than not, however, the bragging rights have belonged to USC fans. The Trojans entered 2005 with a decisive 40–27–7 advantage in the series.

There have been a lot of big games in the USC-UCLA rivalry, but none bigger than the 1967 clash. That year it wasn't just city pride that was on the line. As is often the case (nearly two dozen times through 2004), the winner of the game headed on to the Rose Bowl. On top of that, UCLA entered the game ranked number one in the country and was trying to secure just the second national championship in its history; USC was ranked number four. Plus, Bruins quarterback Gary Beban and Trojans tailback O. J. Simpson were among the leading candidates to win the Heisman Trophy as college football's best player that year.

It was against that backdrop that UCLA forged a 20–14 lead. Beban, though hampered by a rib injury, passed for 301 yards and 2 touchdowns, including a 20-yard strike to Dave Nuttal to break a 14–14 tie early in the fourth quarter. But Xenon Andrushyshyn's extra-point try was blocked, keeping the Bruins' advantage at just 6 points.

O. J.'s Greatest Run

The late Mal Florence, a former walk-on player at USC, a longtime sportswriter for the *Los Angeles Times*, and a Trojan football observer for several decades, used to insist that O. J. Simpson's greatest run wasn't the famous 64-yarder against UCLA in the 1967 game. Rather, it came earlier in the same game: It was his 13-yard touchdown run in the second quarter. On the first run, O. J. didn't have the luxury of the open field that he had on his long score. Instead, he bowled over several Bruin defenders to reach the goal line.

That's when O. J. took over. Simpson was a twenty-year-old junior who had transferred to USC from City College of San Francisco. He made an immediate impact, as the Trojans won their first three games and vaulted to number one in the polls. They stayed there by winning five more times, including a decisive 24–7 victory over fifth-ranked Notre Dame in South Bend.

The Trojans were knocked from their perch by unranked Oregon State the week before the UCLA game. Fullback "Earthquake" Bill Enyart and the Beavers stymied USC in the rain and the mud in Corvallis, 3–0. But Troy quickly recovered and won its sixth national championship by toppling the Bruins on the run that made O. J. famous (for the first time, anyway).

Simpson is among a litany of USC heroes in its series with UCLA. Jim Sears and Al Carmichael, Jimmy Jones, Frank Jordan, George Achica, Rodney Peete, Johnnie Morton, Reggie Bush, and lots of others have had their moments to shine, also.

Sears and Carmichael were the stars when fourth-ranked USC and number-three UCLA met with the Rose Bowl on the line for both teams in 1952. In the first quarter Sears took a lateral from Carmichael and raced 65 yards for a touchdown. In the third quarter, Sears passed for 4 yards to Carmichael for the decisive touchdown in the Trojans' 14–12 triumph.

In 1969 quarterback Jimmy Jones lofted a high, rainbow pass to Sam Dickerson in the back corner of the end zone. Dickerson hauled in the 32-yard strike with 1:32 remaining, and USC was in the Rose Bowl again with another 14–12 victory over the Bruins.

In 1977 it was Frank Jordan's turn. A pair of conference losses already had eliminated the Trojans from the Rose Bowl race, but UCLA needed a win to get in. Jordan's 38-yard field goal with 2 seconds left ended the Bruins' hopes 29–27. (One year later Jordan kicked a 37-yard field goal with 2 seconds to go to beat Notre Dame 27–25.)

In 1981 Heisman Trophy–winning tailback Marcus Allen scooted untouched into the end zone on the go-ahead, 5-yard touchdown run with 2:14 to play against the Bruins. Still, tenth-ranked USC's 22–21 victory over number-fifteen UCLA wasn't secured until George Achica blocked Norm Johnson's 46-yard field goal try as time ran out.

The burly Achica, a 6'5", 260-pound nose guard with the strength of a bear and a heart to match, swatted Johnson's kick back at him and began rumbling off the field to the sidelines, arms raised in joyful celebration. Only one problem: The game

The Trojans have dominated
the Bruins in recent years.
Joe Robbins

was still going on! Because the kick never crossed the line of scrimmage, the ball was still live and could be advanced by the Bruins. No matter. UCLA covered the ball, but a USC player quickly covered him. The Trojans won, knocking the Bruins out of the Rose Bowl.

The Rose Bowl was on the line for the winner again in 1987, when quarterback Rodney Peete made one of the most remarkable plays of his career—as a de facto defender in the game against the Bruins.

Late in the first half, the underdog Trojans trailed fifth-ranked UCLA 10–0 but were driving deep in Bruins territory. Just 14 seconds before intermission, Peete tried to toss a pass into the end zone. But it was tipped at the line of scrimmage and intercepted by UCLA safety Eric Turner at the goal line. Turner raced ahead of the pack in the opposite direction toward an apparent back-breaking touchdown.

Suddenly, here came Peete in a full-out sprint, starting from way back but chasing, chasing . . . "I really believed I was going to catch him," Peete said afterward. "I just didn't know when."

"When" came at the Trojans' 11 yard line and with no time left on the clock. Given a reprieve, USC rallied in the second half to win 17–13. Erik Affholter's juggling, 33-yard touchdown catch midway through the fourth quarter won it.

USC entered 2005 riding a dominating six-game winning streak against UCLA that included some of the most lopsided victories since the schools initially played.

In 2001, for instance, Pete Carroll's first USC team rebounded from a 1–4 start, which included agonizingly close losses to highly ranked Kansas State, Oregon, and Washington, to

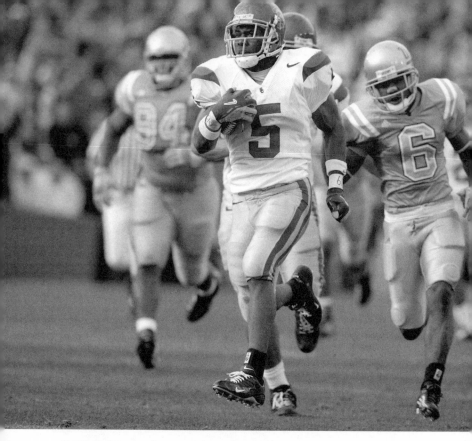

Reggie Bush sprints for a touchdown against UCLA in 2004. Joe Robbins

enter UCLA week riding a three-game winning streak. The Trojans made it four in a row with an overwhelming defensive performance, winning 27–0 at the Coliseum. It was USC's first shutout in the series in fifty-four years.

The next year, Bruin fans headed for the Rose Bowl exits by halftime of the Trojans' 52–21 rout. Carson Palmer helped fuel his Heisman Trophy candidacy by passing for 254 yards and 4 touchdowns, as USC built a 52–7 lead before UCLA broke through for a couple of late touchdowns against the Trojan scrubs.

Roller-coaster Ride

For nonstop thrills, USC's 45–42 victory over UCLA in the 1990 game may be the most memorable in the series. "It was the best game I've ever been associated with," Trojans coach Larry Smith said afterward.

In the highest scoring game in the history of the rivalry, Troy took a 31–21 lead in the fourth quarter, only to see the Bruins rally to a 35–31 advantage behind a pair of touchdown passes from Tommy Maddox to Scott Miller.

USC regained the lead on Todd Marinovich's 21-yard touchdown pass to freshman Johnnie Morton with 3:09 to go, but UCLA countered with a 75-yard drive capped by fullback Kevin Smith's 1-yard touchdown run with just 1:19 to play.

A bleak situation got bleaker when the Trojans immediately faced third down on the ensuing drive. But Marinovich completed a pair of long passes to Gary Wellman, then tossed a 23-yard touchdown pass to a diving Morton in the corner of the end zone for the winning score with 16 seconds left.

It was more of the same in 2003, when USC led 40–2 early in the third quarter before easing up in a 47–22 romp. Freshman tailback Reggie Bush closed the scoring in that one by returning a kickoff 96 yards for a touchdown late in the third quarter.

"We kicked butt," Carroll said afterward, eschewing political correctness but forever endearing himself to Trojan fans.

Bush's big return was a prelude to the 2004 game, in which he broke off two long runs to spark the Trojans to a hard fought

29–24 victory. Bush ran 65 yards for a touchdown on the second play of the game, and later he added an 81-yard scoring jaunt that was reminiscent of Simpson's run in 1967.

It's not just on the field, though, that the USC-UCLA series brings out the best between the two schools. Off the field the series has produced a colorful history of pranks and college hijinks.

Once, in the early 1950s, USC students enlisted the services of a spy at UCLA to sabotage the Bruins' halftime card stunts. Actually, the unwitting UCLA cheering section was unaware of any hitch in the show until newspaper photos the next day revealed small Trojan card stunts within the larger Bruin stunts — the enterprising USC students had replaced a section of cards with their own.

Then there was the time that a group of Trojans burned the letters "USC" into the quad at UCLA. And the time Bruin students shaved "UCLA" onto the back of Trojan mascot George Tirebiter. A group of USC coeds thoughtfully knitted the dog a cardinal-and-gold sweater to cover up the indignity.

USC's Tommy Trojan has been the target of so many Bruin pranks that he is mummified in a protective covering each year the week of the UCLA game. Most of the time the attacks have come in the form of blue-and-gold paint; USC students have returned the favor by painting the Bruin Bear in Westwood cardinal and gold. However, there was the time that a group of Bruins hired a helicopter pilot to hover over the USC landmark while they attempted to dump piles of manure on it. What they didn't figure on, though, was the natural updraft produced by a helicopter's rotors — so that much of the offending material blew right back at them!

Not all of the pranks have been harmless. One year in the 1940s, USC's annual bonfire was ignited early by a pair of UCLA students, creating a potentially hazardous situation. Fortunately, the only injury was to the pride of the two Bruins, who were caught by USC students and had their heads shaved. The shenanigans were getting so out of hand that USC president Rufus B. Von KleinSmid insisted he would cancel the annual series if they didn't stop. They did stop . . . for the most part.

Even the series trophy—the Victory Bell—originated as the result of a prank. In 1939 the UCLA Alumni Association purchased an old locomotive bell from the Southern Pacific Railway and set it on the Bruins sideline during football games. The bell, which weighs nearly 300 pounds, clanged for each point UCLA scored in the 1939 and 1940 seasons. But after the 1941 opener, the bell mysteriously disappeared, having been absconded by several USC fraternity members. The students were so bold that they helped the bell's handlers load it onto a truck bound for Westwood—then swiped the key and sped off when the coast was clear.

For more than a year, the bell was hidden away, until the presidents of the USC and UCLA student bodies signed an agreement to present it annually to the winner of the Trojan-Bruin football game, beginning in 1942, which coincidentally was UCLA's first victory in the series.

Still, the Victory Bell remains in seclusion most of the year. It's rarely seen in public—mostly just on the sidelines of the Los Angeles Coliseum or the Rose Bowl for the first three periods of the USC-UCLA game, and then on the Monday after the game when it returns to the USC campus after a Trojan victory—or on those rarer occasions, after a Bruins win, to Westwood!

Home Away from Home

Traffic permitting (and that's getting rarer and rarer these days), it's only about a thirty-minute drive from the Coliseum near downtown Los Angeles to the Rose Bowl in Pasadena. But for USC fans, each trip to the venerable Arroyo Seco is like a weekend getaway: refreshing, revitalizing—and just right once a year around the holidays.

There's nothing quite like getting up in the early hours of a New Year's morning and finding a seat on the parade route, then sipping hot coffee or cocoa to combat the chill in the air while watching the colorful floats go by. After the parade is over, it's a short walk down the hill into the Rose Bowl, where the Trojans play the Buckeyes (or the Wolverines, or whomever) on what invariably turns into a picture-perfect, chamber-of-commerce day.

Former Michigan head coach Bo Schembechler used to complain that the Trojans' John McKay annually included the Rose Bowl on his team's season schedule. That was only a slight exaggeration: In the nine-season span from 1966 through 1974, McKay's teams played in Pasadena on New Year's Day seven times.

McKay's USC squads won the Rose Bowl five times. John Robinson's Trojan teams won five Rose Bowls, also. Howard Jones didn't lose in his five trips to the Rose Bowl. In all, Troy has won the Rose Bowl twenty-one times—far and away the most of any school. It also represents more wins than any other school has in any other bowl. USC's twenty-nine appearances in the Rose Bowl is another record.

A litany of Rose Bowl records owned by the Trojans, however, is not as telling as the lasting images—generated over more than three quarters of a century—of USC football on New Year's Day.

There's Doyle Nave passing to "Antelope Al" Krueger as dusk descends on the 1939 game, giving the Trojans an upset of Duke . . . Hal Bedsole making a leaping catch in the wild shoot-out with Wisconsin in 1963 . . . Shelton Diggs plucking a two-point conversion—and a national championship—just off the turf in 1975 . . . Charles White diving over the pile for the winning touchdown in 1980 . . . and quarterback Matt Leinart holding the

Johnny McKay made this critical scoring grab against Ohio State in the 1975 Rose Bowl game. AP

ball aloft in the end zone after *catching* a touchdown pass against Michigan in 2004.

Even in the muddled world of the Bowl Championship Series, which has led to a pair of Orange Bowl berths in recent years, there's still only one preferred destination for Trojan fans: "The Rose Bowl is our goal here every year," coach Pete Carroll says.

USC first played in the Rose Bowl on January 1, 1923, a significant event not only because it was Troy's first appearance in the game, but also because it was the first Rose Bowl game played at the current site. USC had christened the stadium by playing the first college game there earlier in the season, losing to California 12–0. The undefeated Golden Bears went on to win the first Pacific Coast Conference title but declined an invitation to play in the Rose Bowl. The 9–1 Trojans gladly accepted and prepared to meet Hugo Bezdek's highly touted Penn State team.

With Pasadena being as it is on New Year's Day (apparently even back then), the Nittany Lions got caught in a traffic jam and arrived at the stadium late. Or so Bezdek said. Conventional belief is that Bezdek didn't want his players, hardened by the harsh winters of the Northeast, boiling under the relatively hot California sun during the intended early afternoon game time. And by the time the game actually kicked off after 3:00 P.M., the sun just happened to be settling behind the San Gabriel Mountains.

No matter. After spotting Penn State an early field goal, USC roared back to win easily 14–3. The late start meant the game finished in the dark, with the *Los Angeles Times* reporting there were so many lit cigars in the stands that they gave the "impression of hundreds of fireflies flitting about the stadium."

The Trojans thus won in their first trip to Pasadena on New Year's Day. It soon would become a habit. USC went on to win each of its first eight appearances in the Rose Bowl, including routs of Pittsburgh in 1930 (47–14) and 1933 (35–0), and consecutive shutouts over Tennessee in 1940 (14–0, the first points scored against the Volunteers in sixteen games), Washington in 1944 (29–0 in the only regional Rose Bowl because of wartime travel restrictions), and Tennessee again in 1945 (25–0).

The only close call came against Duke in 1939, and it provided the Trojans with one of their greatest moments ever. Early in the fourth quarter, Duke broke a scoreless tie when Tony Ruffa kicked a field goal. That figured to be enough for the Blue Devils, who entered the game not only unbeaten and untied, but also unscored upon. They had shut out nine consecutive opponents.

Late in the final period, with USC down to its last chance, head coach Howard Jones looked to the bench—to the far end of his bench—and summoned fourth-string quarterback Doyle Nave. The seldom-used Nave was fourth string for a reason: He wasn't Jones's best quarterback. But he also was a victim of his time, the best passer among Troy's quarterbacks in a non-passing era. Jones knew that; Duke did not.

So when Nave entered the game with the ball on the Blue Devils' 34 yard line and two minutes left, he surprised his opponents by passing four consecutive times. All four were in the direction of end Antelope Al Kruger, and all four were complete, including a 19-yard strike for the decisive touchdown with 40 seconds remaining.

Trojan fans were delirious. In the last minute of the last game of the season, USC scored the only points Duke allowed all season. *Los Angeles Times* sports editor Braven Dyer unabashedly called USC's 7–3 victory "the most spectacular triumph in all Trojan history!"

"Nave is without a peer as a passer," Krueger said after the game. But Nave had played the equivalent of only about one half a game all season—far short of the requirements for a letterman. "I wonder if I'll get that letter, anyway," he mused to trainer Doc Thurber in the locker room after the game. He got the letter.

Quarterback Jim Hardy had his letter wrapped up long before the Trojans' 1945 Rose Bowl showdown with Tennessee. The Volunteers entered the game unbeaten, but Hardy passed for 2 touchdowns and ran for another to pace USC's 25–0 rout. The

Trash Talk

The late start and the late finish to the 1923 Rose Bowl—indeed, reporters had to light matches to type their game accounts—gave rise to a legendary story that has grown over time.

For many years, it's been reported that USC head coach "Gloomy Gus" Henderson and Penn State coach Hugo Bezdek nearly came to blows on the field prior to the game and exchanged vicious barbs after the game because of the Nittany Lions' late arrival.

"My only regret is that Elmer Henderson left his glasses on," Bezdek is quoted as saying. "Thank God for the guy who made it a criminal offense to hit a man wearing glasses," the bespectacled Henderson said.

"The best team lost," Bezdek reportedly whined after the game. "The best team and the best coaching in the world couldn't have won against the luck that USC had today."

"Good coaching always tells in the long run," Henderson countered. "We should have won by 4 more touchdowns."

The only problem with this delightful repartee is that it didn't actually happen. Because of the game's finish in the dark, reporters

Trojans took the lead only four plays into the game when end Jim Callahan blocked a punt and returned it 38 yards for the fastest touchdown in Rose Bowl history.

Two years later, the Pac-10 (then the Pacific Coast Conference) and the Big Ten (it really did have ten teams at the time)

with impending deadlines were not able to run down to the field or to the locker rooms to obtain any quotes from the participants. So one enterprising journalist simply made them up.

As outlandish as that sounds, it was merely an attempt at humor. In fact, the *Los Angeles Times* admitted in its copy that the quotes were generated by a "cub" reporter and intended to serve as "official" quotes. And while that part of the story has gotten lost over the years, the outrageous nature of the remarks themselves should be enough to give them away. Consider a couple more postgame gems, such as USC guard Leo Calland proclaiming himself the "star of the game." Or this brilliant one from a Penn State player: "Coach Bezdek probably means well, but I think he is a good baseball coach."

That last one is particularly clever because Bezdek also had been the manager of Major League Baseball's Pittsburgh Pirates from 1917 to 1919. In fact, Bezdek, who went on to become the first head coach of pro football's Cleveland Rams in 1937 (his team won only one of fourteen games before he was let go in 1938), is the answer to a trivia question: He is the only man to serve both as a head coach in the NFL and a manager in Major League Baseball.

entered into their historic agreement to have their champions play in the Rose Bowl each year. By 1953 the West Coast teams still were looking for their first win. USC finally delivered it, with Rudy Bukich's 22-yard touchdown pass to Al "Hoagy" Carmichael providing the only points in a 7–0 triumph.

Double Duty

Who was the first man to have played on and coached a winning team in the Rose Bowl? The answer: USC's Jess Hill. He was a fullback on Troy's 1929 team, which routed Pittsburgh 47–14 in the Rose Bowl on New Year's Day 1930. Hill later coached the 1952 Trojans to a 7–0 victory over Wisconsin on New Year's Day 1953.

John McKay took a team to the Rose Bowl for the first time in the 1962 season. At 10–0, the Trojans had already wrapped up the national championship (at the time, the final polls were released before the bowl games). They validated it with a 42–37 triumph over second-ranked Wisconsin in the 1963 Rose Bowl.

The game is best remembered for the brilliant play of Badgers quarterback Ron VanderKelen, who passed for 401 yards and 2 touchdowns while completing 33 of 48 attempts and nearly rallying his team to victory. Lost in the praise for VanderKelen, though, was USC's Pete Beathard, who completed only 8 passes, but 4 were for touchdowns. End Hal Bedsole caught two of Beathard's scoring tosses to help the Trojans build a 42–14 lead in the fourth quarter—an advantage that proved insurmountable.

Several Trojan players were miffed after the game that the media was more intent on talking about Wisconsin's comeback than USC's win. "I'll tell you what happened," halfback Willie Brown said after the game. "We won!"

"Our intention was to win today," McKay said. "And what does the scoreboard say?"

McKay and the Trojans lost the 1967 Rose Bowl game to Purdue, 14–13. But it was noteworthy for an important philosophical stand by the coach. USC trailed 14–7 until scoring a touchdown with 2:28 left in the game to pull within 1 point. McKay eschewed the tie, opting instead to go for the win with a two-point conversion. Troy Winslow's pass for Jim Lawrence was intercepted by George Catavalos, and the Boilermakers hung on to win.

The try may have been no good, but McKay's point was made. "We always go for the win," he said. "There were fifty-eight million people who watched the game, and they didn't want us to play for a tie."

That stance eventually carried USC to a national championship. It came in the 1974 season, the last time that McKay took a team to the Rose Bowl. Less than five weeks after USC's dramatic, 55–24 comeback victory over Notre Dame, the Trojans won another thriller for the all-time highlight reel, outlasting third-ranked Ohio State 18–17.

With just over two minutes remaining and USC trailing 17–10, quarterback Pat Haden dropped back from the Buckeyes' 38 yard line and lofted a rainbow pass high into the corner of the end zone in the direction of Johnny McKay. The coach's son hauled in the toss to make it 17–16.

Once again, the elder McKay never wavered. Amid the bedlam in the stands and on the sidelines, he called for a two-point conversion attempt. Haden took the snap, sprinted right, and looked for McKay again in the end zone. But with McKay being double covered, "I decided to run," Haden said.

This two-point conversion catch by Shelton Diggs in the 1975 Rose Bowl game gave USC a national title. AP

The Buckeyes' defense figured that out pretty quick and came up to meet Haden. That's when Haden saw Shelton Diggs alone in the back of the end zone, his defender having deserted him to go after the quarterback. Diggs grabbed Haden's low pass just before it hit the turf and held the ball aloft for all to see.

"The difference was that much," Ohio State coach Woody Hayes said after the game, two fingers almost touching. He meant the difference in the game, but he could have meant the difference in the national championship.

This was the first year that the coaches awarded the UPI national title after the bowl games were played. With the Associated Press champion, Oklahoma, on probation and ineligible to win the UPI crown, the door was open for undefeated Alabama to win it on New Year's night. But Notre Dame, which had its title hopes crushed by USC's comeback at the Coliseum on November 30, upset the Crimson Tide 13–11.

The next day the 10–1–1 Trojans learned that their victory over the Buckeyes had lifted them to the national championship. Alabama finished second, Ohio State third, and Notre Dame fourth.

Three years later USC finished second in the polls, but another legend was born. The Trojans beat Michigan 14–6 in the 1977 Rose Bowl, winning their eleventh consecutive game after losing the 1976 opener to Missouri in John Robinson's first game as coach. One of the stars of the game was tailback Charles White, who came off the bench to replace injured starter Ricky Bell early in the first quarter.

White, a true freshman, ran for 114 yards, including a 7-yard touchdown. The game officially marked the beginning of his emergence as one of Troy's all-time great tailbacks. The end came three years later, when White capped his Heisman Trophy–winning season with one of the most memorable individual performances in the Rose Bowl.

That year third-ranked USC trailed top-rated Ohio State 16–10 in the fourth quarter on New Year's Day. Starting from their 17 yard line with 5:21 left, the Trojans stunned the Buckeyes by driving 83 yards in eight plays—with all of the yardage coming on the ground.

"Give me the ball," White implored quarterback Paul McDonald when the Trojans entered the huddle on the last drive. On first down, McDonald gave it to him, and White rumbled 32 yards. On the next play, McDonald gave it to him again, and White went for 28 yards. Two plays, 60 yards. Already, USC was at Ohio State's 23 yard line.

With White (who had been battling flu-like symptoms) catching his breath on the sidelines for two plays, Michael Hayes carried for 7 yards and Marcus Allen for 5. The ball was at the 11. After that, it was all White. Runs of 3, 5, and 2 yards for a first down at the 1 were followed by a spectacular over-the-top dive into the end zone for the touchdown with 1:32 left.

USC kept the Buckeyes from making a first down on the ensuing possession, and the Trojans held on to win 17–16. "That's our style," White said afterward. "We wear people down."

That's for sure. In addition to the blocking of Allen (the fullback who would move to tailback the next season and in 1981 become a Heisman winner himself), White ran behind a massive and athletic offensive line that included tackle Anthony Muñoz, who would go on to become one of the NFL's all-time greats.

Muñoz had been injured in the opening game of the season against Texas Tech and had not played since. Though healthy for the Rose Bowl, friends and scouts urged him to skip the game so as not to risk another injury or jeopardize his draft chances with a poor outing.

Indeed, most of the yardage on the decisive drive came from running directly behind Muñoz, who not only solidified his status for the following spring's NFL draft but actually enhanced it. Cincinnati Bengals assistant general manager Mike Brown laughed aloud while watching the Rose Bowl from the stands.

"The guy was so big and so good, it was a joke," Brown said. The Bengals soon selected Muñoz with the third pick of the draft.

White, who would go on to star in the NFL himself, became the first player to rush for 200 yards in the Rose Bowl, finishing that day with 247. Not surprisingly he was named the player of the game.

Going Bowling

USC's bowl history is not limited to the Rose Bowl. In all, the Trojans have appeared in a dozen different bowls covering forty-three games. And with 28 postseason victories, Troy ranks second only to Alabama (29) in all-time bowl wins. The Trojans have not had quite the success in bowls outside of Pasadena that they've had in the "Granddaddy of Them All." Here's how USC has fared in bowl games other than the Rose Bowl (the year listed corresponds to the actual calendar date):

1924	Christmas Festival	USC 20, Missouri 7
1975	Liberty Bowl	USC 20, Texas A & M 0
1977	Bluebonnet Bowl	USC 47, Texas A & M 28
1982	Fiesta Bowl	Penn State 26, USC 10
1985	Aloha Bowl	Alabama 24, USC 3
1987	Florida Citrus Bowl	Auburn 16, USC 7
1990	John Hancock Bowl	Michigan State 17, USC 16
1992	Freedom Bowl	Fresno State 24, USC 7
1993	Freedom Bowl	USC 28, Utah 21
1995	Cotton Bowl	USC 55, Texas Tech 14
1998	Sun Bowl	TCU 28, USC 19
2001	Las Vegas Bowl	Utah 10, USC 6
2003	Orange Bowl	USC 38, Iowa 17
2005	Orange Bowl	USC 55, Oklahoma 19

The next time a Trojan tailback was named the player of the game in the Rose Bowl was in 1990, when Ricky Ervins gained 170 yards from scrimmage in USC's 17–10 victory over Michi-

Quarterback Matt Leinart exults in the 2004 Rose Bowl game. Nam Y. Huh/AP

gan. Ervins broke a 10–10 tie by running 14 yards for a touch-down with 1:10 left to play.

Just five years earlier, the Pasadena resident had parked cars at the Rose Bowl before USC's 20–17 victory over Ohio State. On that day twelve-year-old Keyshawn Johnson was a Trojan ball boy. Johnson would go on to become one of the greatest wide receivers in school history. He earned game MVP honors by catching 12 passes for a Rose Bowl–record 216 yards in USC's 41–32 victory over number-three Northwestern on New Year's Day 1996.

Quarterback Matt Leinart was the MVP of USC's 28–14 victory over Michigan in the 2004 Rose Bowl. The left-hander completed 23 of 34 passes for 327 yards and 3 touchdowns, as the top-ranked Trojans wrapped up the Associated Press's half of the national championship with a decisive victory over the fourth-ranked Wolverines.

The most memorable play of the game, however, wasn't one of Leinart's passes but his lone reception. From Michigan's 15 yard line, Leinart handed off to running back Hershel Dennis, who handed the ball to wide receiver Mike Williams on an apparent reverse. Instead Williams tossed a perfect strike to Leinart streaking to the end zone to give USC a 28–7 lead late in the third quarter.

Legends and Lore

USC has won more than 700 college football games in over a century of play. The school has claimed eleven national championships and produced six Heisman Trophy winners. But the Trojans' gridiron history is a lot more than just a litany of names and numbers. It is also composed of the many colorful characters who have worn the cardinal and gold over the decades. Here are some of their stories:

The hero of USC's famous 16–14 upset of Notre Dame in 1931 almost didn't make it to South Bend that year. Routine air travel was still many years away then, so the Trojans and their contingent—including the soon-to-be-legendary Johnny Baker—boarded a train for Indiana several days before the game against the Fighting Irish. Just as Notre Dame often did on its way out west, USC stopped in Tucson on its way east to get in some practice time under the warm Arizona sun.

But Baker, a guard who had been nursing an injured knee, had a hard time getting back into the swing of things after missing Troy's previous two games. USC head coach Howard Jones, always a stern taskmaster who allowed no excuses, let him have it.

A frustrated Baker nearly turned right around and headed back to Los Angeles. "I came within a whisker of quitting the team right then and there," Baker later confided to veteran sportswriter Braven Dyer in a story relayed by author Ken Rappoport.

Lucky for USC, Baker continued on to South Bend. His 33-yard field goal with a minute remaining in the game erased the last of the Trojans' 14-point deficit and gave them one of college football's stunning upsets.

. . .

One of the most famous players in USC history really wasn't much of a player at all. Marion Morrison was a reserve tackle for the Trojans in 1925 and 1926, but he didn't see enough playing time to earn a varsity letter either of those two seasons. (An off-season shoulder injury ended any chance he had of significant playing time in 1926.)

But while Morrison wasn't a star at USC, he soon became a big one. That's because Marion Morrison eventually was known to millions of people around the world by his motion picture screen name: John Wayne.

. . .

Nestled in Los Angeles only a few miles from Hollywood, it's little wonder that some of Hollywood's biggest names are USC alumni. Actors and actresses such as John Wayne, Ron Howard, John Ritter, Tom Selleck, and Marlo Thomas studied there, as well as directors and producers such as Paul Mazursky, Barney Rosenzweig, David Wolper, and Robert Zemeckis. The university's School of Cinema-Television includes the George Lucas Instructional Building, named for the *Star Wars* creator and former USC student.

Trojan football stars have gotten into the act, also. In 1929 John Wayne returned to campus to recruit USC players to join him for the football scenes in director John Ford's *Salute*. (Wayne later starred for Ford in a number of Westerns, including the one that really made him a star, *Stagecoach*, in 1939.)

One of the Trojans on that 1929 squad was Ward Bond, a three-year tackle who became a close friend of Wayne's and went on to a long career himself in the movies. Bond appeared in hundreds of films, but he is probably most famous for his role as Major Seth Adams in television's *Wagon Train*, in which he starred from 1957 until his death of a heart attack at age fifty-seven in 1960.

From 1956 to 1958 Mike Henry lettered at tackle for USC. In the late 1960s he starred as Tarzan in three films but turned down the role on television after suffering various maladies during shooting, including a severe bite from a chimpanzee.

The Duke

John Wayne once earned a game ball from USC, but it was long after his playing career ended. Wayne remained a Trojan football fan after becoming a Hollywood star, and he dropped in on USC games whenever his shooting schedule allowed. In 1966, the Trojans opened the season against Texas in Austin, and Wayne was there.

Before the game he asked to address the players. Inspired by the presence of the living legend in their locker room and on the sideline, ninth-ranked USC beat the Longhorns 10–6. The Trojans sealed the victory by running out the last eight minutes of the fourth quarter after a Texas punt pinned them at their 2 yard line.

After the game head coach John McKay presented Wayne with the game ball. The Duke was speechless. "It was probably the first time in his life that he couldn't think of anything to say," Trojan administrator Nick Pappas told author Ken Rappoport.

Irvine "Cotton" Warburton, an All-America back for the Trojans in 1933, went on to a career as a highly respected film editor. He won an Academy Award for his editing on 1964's *Mary Poppins*.

Nick Pappas, who had a long and distinguished career as a USC player, assistant coach, and administrator, didn't earn any billings in Hollywood, but he played a big role in a major motion picture. Pappas was actor Pat O'Brien's double for football scenes in 1940's *Knute Rockne: All American*, the film in which O'Brien played Rockne and Ronald Reagan played George Gipp.

. . .

Another former Trojan who is recognizable as a character actor on television and in the movies is Tim Rossovich, a defensive end for USC from 1965 to 1967 (he was a consensus All-America choice as a senior). Rossovich went on to play seven seasons in the NFL with the Philadelphia Eagles, San Diego Chargers, and Houston Oilers, then he turned to acting. He starred in several motion pictures and in dozens of shows on television.

Rossovich earned a reputation as a zany character who would do just about anything to gain attention or win a bet. At USC—where one of his roommates was future actor Tom Selleck—that meant typical college shenanigans, such as swallowing goldfish or driving his sports car up his fraternity house steps and into the house for dinner.

"I look back sometimes and think maybe it would have been better to go the straight and narrow," he said. "But remember, this was the sixties and seventies, and I don't think I ever did anything that was really a problem or an embarrassment to the university. It was just hijinks."

And one-upsmanship. "So someone had a goldfish and I ate the goldfish," Rossovich said. "I thought, 'Okay, that was kind of gross,' but then I drank the water. And then I ate the bowl. It was just one step more to be better. I was just searching for excellence, I guess!"

. . .

There's little question that Tim Rossovich marched to the beat of his own drummer. He once relayed a bizarre, recurring dream he used to have.

"I was playing in the Super Bowl," he said, "and the stadium was so big that you couldn't even see the fans in the end zones. They were up in the clouds. It was kind of like the Rose Bowl, except that it held about a million people."

The game in Rossovich's dream came down to the closing seconds. His team held a 4-point lead, but the opponents drove to the 1 yard line with time enough for just one more play.

"I was playing middle linebacker," Rossovich said, "and the fullback got the ball and dove over the line, and we hit helmets. His head explodes and we land on the 1 foot line. We win the game and the fans go crazy. But we're both mortally wounded. I get up and walk out to the 50 yard line and give everyone this wave, and then I drop dead. Then my spirit comes out of my body, I disappear into the clouds, and the fans hush. That's my exit." Rossovich's actual exit from football was more conventional. He retired after playing in fourteen games for the Houston Oilers in 1976.

. . .

Contrary to popular belief—a belief he tongue-in-cheek perpetuated—former USC player and longtime assistant coach Marv Goux did not pose for Tommy Trojan. "For years and years he told kids he did," said Tim Rossovich, who was recruited by Goux in the mid-1960s.

In truth, the famous bronze sculpture that long has been a popular meeting place in the center of the USC campus was created by Roger Noble Burnham from a composite of several Trojan players from the 1920s, most notably backs Russ Saunders and Erny Pinckert. "You see my head, chest, and shoulders," Saunders said. "The rest is all Erny."

But no Goux. The statue was unveiled for USC's 50th Jubilee in 1930, and any enterprising player or recruit easily could have discovered that Goux didn't play until the 1950s. Still, "Coach Goux could have posed for the statue," Rossovich said. "He was the heart and soul of the university."

. . .

Marv Goux was USC's inspirational leader while a longtime assistant coach from 1957 to 1982. He was the genuine article, a man who could get as fired up for a preseason scrimmage in August as for the Rose Bowl on New Year's Day. But nothing got Goux's heart racing and his gravelly voice roaring quite like the USC–Notre Dame rivalry.

"As a youngster, my hero was Johnny Lujack [Notre Dame's 1947 Heisman Trophy–winning quarterback]," said Goux, who grew up in Santa Barbara. "He once was on a *Life* magazine cover, and I remember cutting that out and putting it above my bed frame. My dad loved Notre Dame. We'd go to the same motion picture show over and over and stay until the end just so he could see Notre Dame again on the newsreel."

After graduating from Santa Barbara High School, Goux decided he wanted to play against the Irish. He eventually did, lettering at USC in 1952, 1954, and 1955. "I wanted to play major college football, I wanted to play in a Rose Bowl, and I wanted to play Notre Dame," Goux said. "So for me, USC was the only place to go."

. . .

The familiar trumpet fanfare "Charge," heard at sporting events all over the United States these days ("Da-da-da-dat-da-daa . . . Charge!"), was the brainchild of USC band member Tommy Walker in 1946.

Walker had just come back from serving in World War II when he penned the brief fanfare. It was a big hit at Trojan games, then it became nationally famous after baseball's Dodgers borrowed it following their move to the West Coast in 1958.

Walker, who graduated in 1948, eventually became USC's band director and then the first entertainment director at Disneyland before starting his own production company. His contributions to Trojan football were not limited to those from the stands, though. In 1947 Tommy walked on to the team as a kicker. Believe it or not, he didn't have to give up his duties in the band. Because he only kicked, Walker did not don pads with his football uniform, which he wore under his band garb. When USC scored a touchdown, he would shed his band uniform and run down to the field to kick the extra point. He made 19 conversions that year, a conference record at the time.

. . .

Tailback O. J. Simpson arrived at USC in 1967 from Galileo High School in San Francisco, after a two-year stop at City College of San Francisco. At the time O.J. wasn't the most famous athlete to come out of the San Francisco prep school. He had been preceded at Galileo by baseball legend Joe DiMaggio and basketball star Hank Luisetti.

Galileo can boast of having produced some of the greatest professionals in the three major sports. DiMaggio, Luisetti, and Simpson all are in their respective sports' halls of fame.

. . .

In all, ten former Trojan players are enshrined in the Pro Football Hall of Fame in Canton, Ohio: running back Marcus Allen, end Red Badgro, halfback Frank Gifford, defensive back Ronnie Lott, tackle Ron Mix, tackle Anthony Muñoz, running back O. J. Simpson, wide receiver Lynn Swann, defensive back Willie Wood, and tackle Ron Yary.

. . .

"Cotton" Warburton is just one of a number of colorful nicknames in USC's history. He got his nickname for his tow-headed appearance, including a head of light colored hair. Warburton played in the same era as stars such as "Amblin' Amby" Schindler, "Field Marshall" Duffield, "Racehorse Russ" Saunders, and "Blackjack" Harry Smith. Later came "Antelope Al" Krueger and "Jaguar Jon" Arnett.

Three-time All-American linebacker Richard Wood was known as "Batman" because of his prodigious arm span. Wood patrolled the middle of the USC defense from 1972 to 1974—not long after the campy superhero enjoyed his original three-year run on American television.

Perhaps the most famous nickname is "The Noblest Trojan of Them All," a regal moniker reserved for 1920s quarterback Morley Drury. A consensus All-America selection in 1927, when he rushed for 1,163 yards—in the days when 1,000-yard rushers were almost nonexistent—Drury had the name bestowed on him by a local sportswriter. Drury, who played a position that more closely resembles today's tailback than quarterback, was one of the Trojans' first national stars. After his 1,000-yard rushing season, it was thirty-eight years before another USC player (tailback Mike Garrett in 1965) reached that magical plateau.

. . .

Head coach Howard Jones was known as the "Headman," because he left little doubt about who was in charge of the Trojans' football program during his tenure from 1925 to 1940. Jones succeeded "Gloomy Gus" Henderson, Troy's coach from 1919 to 1924.

Gloomy Gus was the Lou Holtz of his time, always downplaying USC's chances while elevating opposing teams to powerhouse status. But Henderson's Trojans were rarely overmatched, as evidenced by their remarkable 45–7 record during his tenure as coach.

Henderson got his name from the popular *Happy Hooligan* comic strip of the time. Gloomy Gus was the title character's brother and the pessimistic antithesis to Happy's optimist. That's where the modern notion of a Gloomy Gus comes from, also.

. . .

The 1968 Trojans were called the "Cardiac Kids" after enduring several close calls en route to a 9–0–1 record during the regular season. Troy pulled out three consecutive midseason games in the fourth quarter; later, the top-ranked Trojans scored all of their points in a 17–13 win over Oregon State in the final period.

Then they tied number-nine Notre Dame 21–21 with a fourth-quarter touchdown.

It was more of the same in 1969, when USC outlasted three opponents with dramatic scores inside of two minutes, including UCLA, on Jimmy Jones's 32-yard rainbow pass to Sam Dickerson in the corner of the end zone with 1:32 left. A 7-point win over Michigan in the Rose Bowl capped Troy's 10–0–1 season.

That team also featured the "Wild Bunch," a collective nickname given to USC's dominating defensive line of Al Cowlings, Jimmy Gunn, Willard Scott, Tody Smith, Tony Terry, and Charlie Weaver. The name was derived from the motion picture of the same name—a popular but violent movie by the standards of the 1960s—for the havoc that the line created for the Trojans' opponents.

"Wild Bunch II" followed more than thirty years later—not in theaters, but along USC's defensive line. Kenechi Udeze, Shaun Cody, Mike Patterson, and Omar Nazel helped the Trojans go 12–1 and win the national championship in 2003.

・ ・ ・

Talk about the most famous streaks in sports history: Joe DiMaggio's 56 consecutive games with a hit . . . Johnny Unitas's 47 consecutive games with a touchdown pass . . . the Lakers' 33 wins in a row. They all pale in comparison, however, to the most famous streak in USC's football history: Giles Pellerin's 797 consecutive games in the stands.

You read that right—797 consecutive games. Beginning with Troy's season opener in 1926, when he was a USC sophomore, Pellerin saw every Trojan football game until he passed away in November of 1998. That's home and away games, regular season games and bowls, games all around the United States and beyond. (USC played a game in Tokyo to close the regular season in 1985, and Pellerin was there.) A Trojan fan seeing his or her first game in 2005 would have to see every game into the 2070s to break it.

A phone company executive in his professional life, Pellerin earned the nickname "Super Fan" for his passionate devotion. He was there for the first USC–Notre Dame game in December 1926 and for the first USC-UCLA clash in September 1929.

Late in his life Pellerin confided that "going to USC games is the thing that has kept me alive, young, and happy." His death at age ninety-one came doing what he loved most: watching USC and UCLA play at the Coliseum. A lot of sports streaks are considered unbreakable, but the reality is that most of them will fall one day. But Super Fan's streak is one that almost certainly will never be broken.

. . .

USC's first All-American was guard Brice Taylor in 1925. At first glance a publicity photo of Taylor looks like most of the surviving shots of the day: a posed, three-point stance on the Trojan practice field. But look a little closer. Taylor's right hand rests on the grass. His left hand . . . well, he was born without a left hand.

Taylor never let the disability slow him down—literally. A speedster who was a member of USC's world record–setting mile relay team, he utilized his quickness to become a devastating blocker and tackler despite standing only 5'9" and weighing 185 pounds.

Taylor had to overcome one other significant obstacle in his career: He was a black player in an era when black players often were not welcomed. It would be more than twenty years before African-America players shattered the color barrier in the NFL and longer than that before African-Americans were welcomed at many universities, particularly in the South. No other black player earned All-America honors at USC until tailback Mike Garrett in the mid-1960s.

. . .

USC helped integrate football in the South on a visit to Alabama in 1970. The culturally diverse Trojans took the field in Birmingham against legendary coach Bear Bryant's all-white Crimson Tide to open the season that year.

With African-American fullback Sam "Bam" Cunningham leading the way, third-ranked USC routed number-sixteen Alabama 42–21. After the game Bryant sought out Cunningham and brought him into the Crimson Tide's locker room. "Men, this is what a football player looks like," Bryant told his team.

That sounds terribly patronizing today, but the legendary coach's point was made. By the next time that USC and Alabama played in 1977, Bryant's squad was integrated—and most schools in the South had followed suit. That year the seventh-ranked Crimson Tide upset the Trojans, who had ascended to the top spot in the polls only several days earlier, 21–20.

. . .

In 1988 quarterback Rodney Peete walked out of the hospital and into Trojan football lore when he led USC past UCLA 31–22. Maybe it wasn't exactly out of the hospital (he had practiced the day before the game) and maybe it wasn't a debilitating injury (though measles in an adult can have serious complications), but once he stepped onto the Rose Bowl field on Saturday, it was as

Quarterback Rodney Peete (16) celebrates against UCLA in 1988. *Mark Terrill/AP*

if he was Willis Reed hobbling out to center court to inspire the Knicks past the Lakers in the NBA Finals.

That's because Peete's uncertain status in the days leading up to the game had much of the Cardinal and Gold section of Los Angeles wringing its collective hands with worry. He had been instrumental in directing the ninth-ranked Trojans to a 9–0 record heading into their showdown with the number-six Bruins, who were 9–1. The winner would head to the Rose Bowl and keep its national championship hopes alive.

Though Rodney didn't have to do a whole lot in this game—tailback Aaron Emanuel supplied much of the offense by running for 135 yards and 2 touchdowns—his presence alone helped carry the Trojans to a relatively easy 31–22 victory. A 29-yard touchdown pass to Erik Affholter to help open a 14–3 lead didn't hurt, either.

. . .

As good a football player as Rodney Peete was—and he was a very good one—he may have been an even better baseball player. He was a terrific hitter who could hit for average or power, had a terrific glove, and possessed great baseball instincts.

Truth is, Rodney, who now is married to actress Holly Robinson-Peete, is one of those guys who can probably succeed at just about anything he chooses. He always has a smile on his face and a way of making everyone feel good about themselves—a born leader.

After USC he chose football over baseball. He was still active through 2004, having completed his sixteenth NFL season with the Carolina Panthers.

. . .

The school known for producing so many Heisman Trophy winners also boasts the alum who started the "Lowsman" Trophy. Paul Salata was an end for USC in the 1940s who went on to play two years in the NFL with the San Francisco 49ers and Baltimore Colts. He remained active in the league's alumni affairs, and in 1976 he decided to honor the last player selected in the NFL draft. He called him "Mr. Irrelevant," and over the course of more than a quarter century, the tongue-in-cheek award grew to include an entire "Irrelevant Week" full of fun.

Irrelevant Week's motto is: "Doing something nice for someone for no reason." Most of the players have fun with it, and the

Child's Play

NFL wide receiver Keyshawn Johnson was a star at USC in the mid-1990s, but he was a fixture at the university long before that. As a youngster who grew up not far from the school, Keyshawn often could be found at football practice, joking with players and coaches or hanging around the sports information department. It's not hard to imagine what Keyshawn was like as a kid. He was cocky but good natured, and he almost always had that trademark grin on his face.

"You know Keyshawn—always going, always talking," says Dave Rush, the senior manager for USC's 1978 team. "He was that way even then. It got to the point where we had to find something for him to do."

So Rush sent him outside the practice field to a school intramural field. There, six-year-old Keyshawn caught the balls that place-kickers booted through the uprights and over the fence at Howard Jones Field while practicing field goals. Rush laughs. "I don't think I've ever gotten any credit for some of his earliest experience catching footballs!"

week's proceeds benefits various charities in Southern California. Mr. Irrelevant is presented with the Lowsman Trophy, which depicts a player fumbling the football. While the Trojans have produced six Heisman Trophy winners, they've yet to have anyone take home the Lowsman.

. . .

After USC's stunning 55–24 comeback victory over Notre Dame in 1974, quarterback Pat Haden couldn't contain his enthusiasm. "I was so excited, I went home and asked my future wife to marry me," Haden said.

A quarter of a century later, another USC quarterback popped the question after USC's final home game. Only this time, John Fox did it immediately after the game, pulling his girlfriend aside and asking her to marry him while still on the field following the Trojans' 45–19 victory over Louisiana Tech in 1999.

The moment was captured on the Coliseum video board. To the delight of Fox's teammates and the fans in the stands, she said yes. They don't call it the "Trojan Family" for nothing.

Pete Carroll and a Return to Glory

If Pete Carroll were the vindictive sort, he could have stood on the postgame dais that was hurriedly assembled following the 2005 Orange Bowl and thumbed his nose at the critics. He could have given a collective raspberry to all the letter writers and sports talk hosts and columnists who assailed USC for his hiring in December of 2000.

Fortunately Carroll is not the vindictive sort. Instead he basked in the glow of the top-ranked Trojans' 55–19 thrashing of number-two Oklahoma in the BCS title game, flashing the victory sign, leading the band, and generally enjoying himself. "How much do we love this!" he shouted to the Trojan fans who stayed in the stands long after the game had ended to celebrate.

Trojan fans love it a lot. Before Carroll's arrival for the 2001 season, USC had spent much of the previous two decades trying to recapture the glory years of the 1960s and 1970s under John McKay and John Robinson. Troy went through a series of head coaches—including Robinson again—before hiring Carroll in 2001. Previously Carroll had only moderate success as an NFL coach, and he was far from the school's first choice. But his unlimited energy and enthusiasm quickly proved to be a perfect fit at USC, and his second squad won eleven games and earned a Bowl Championship Series berth. His third team, in 2003, won a share of the national championship. And his fourth left no doubt, winning the BCS title game and earning nearly unanimous (as in pretty much anyone outside of Auburn, Alabama) acclaim as the best team in the nation.

The Orange Bowl victory gave Troy its second consecutive national championship and its eleventh overall. It also gave USC thirteen wins in a season for the first time ever, capped the school's first perfect season since the great 1972 team, and extended the Trojans' winning streak to twenty-two games, the best in the nation entering 2005.

Few people, not even the most ardent Trojan fans and not even the most ardent Carroll supporters—athletic director Mike Garrett (the man who hired him) and associate athletic director Daryl Gross (the man who conducted the search)—could have envisioned USC's return to glory in so rapid and so dramatic a fashion. Truth is, some of the more ardent Trojan fans were some of the more vocal critics when Carroll was hired.

"A repackaging of Paul Hackett," wrote one in a letter to the editor in the *Los Angeles Times*. "A net loss [from Hackett to Carroll]," wrote another. And, "Somewhere [then-UCLA coach] Bob Toledo must be smiling."

Certainly after each move in the coaching search was scrutinized daily for nearly three weeks, it appeared as if USC simply settled for Carroll. And the truth is, he was not Garrett's first choice as coach. He was not the second, either. Maybe not even the third.

When the administration decided it had seen enough of the disorganized mess that characterized the Paul Hackett era shortly after a 38–21 rout by Notre Dame ended a 5–7 season in 2000, Garrett began wooing Mike Bellotti, the coach at Oregon. Bellotti was the hottest commodity in the conference after leading the Ducks to five bowls in his first six seasons at the school. But— perhaps knowing that Garrett would turn him down—Bellotti reportedly demanded a contract and perks for his assistants that were deemed outrageous.

So Garrett turned to Oregon State coach Dennis Erickson, a man who previously had guided Miami to a pair of national championships and led the moribund Beavers to an 11–1 record and a Fiesta Bowl rout over Notre Dame to close the 2000 season. Garrett offered him the job, but Erickson turned it down.

The Trojans interviewed Colorado State coach Sonny Lubick, then tried to woo San Diego Chargers coach Mike Riley. A former USC assistant, Riley wanted the job . . . then he

Happy days are here
again for Trojan football
under Pete Carroll.
Joe Robbins

didn't . . . then he did. But in any case he was contractually obligated to the NFL club for another three years, and the Chargers didn't want to let him go (though they eventually fired him the next season).

Meanwhile Carroll began campaigning for the job. Three years earlier, before Hackett was hired, Carroll had spurned an offer from Garrett. He was completing a 10–6 season in his first year as head coach of the NFL's New England Patriots, and "the timing wasn't right," he said. But in 2000, after a year out of coaching and with a daughter enrolled at the university, the timing was right. Carroll was hired as the Trojans' football coach on December 15.

Reaction was swift and immediate. By December 16 the general consensus was that the Trojans had hired another Hackett: a successful NFL coordinator (on the defensive side this time instead of the offensive side) who had failed in his only previous stints as a head coach (never mind that he didn't have a losing season in three years with the Patriots and took two of his squads to the playoffs).

Plus Carroll didn't have recruiting ties, had no staff ready to go, and hadn't coached in college since he was the offensive coordinator at Pacific in 1983. "I've always coached college kids," he countered with a smile. "I just got them a little later."

Garrett knew he would be criticized for the move, though the vitriol was startling, nevertheless. "I'm mad at USC for hiring him," one *Los Angeles Times* columnist wrote.

But Carroll, who had stepped into a difficult situation before (he succeeded the popular Bill Parcells as coach in New England), immediately began winning over the critics with his energy and enthusiasm—traits that his detractors didn't realize would translate as well to the college atmosphere as they did.

"The enthusiasm he exudes was greeted with cynicism here in New England," said Jim Donaldson, a columnist for the *Providence Journal* during Carroll's stint with the Patriots. "But it works tremendously well in the college ranks. And obviously on the recruiting trail."

"His style fits the college game," said former USC linebacker Willie McGinest, who played for Carroll in New England. "They'll love him."

McGinest turned out to be prescient. Only weeks after officially taking the helm, Carroll landed a prize recruit in prep All-America defensive lineman Shaun Cody, who had been considering the likes of Notre Dame, Washington, and UCLA. Tailback Justin Fargas, who had passed up a chance to attend USC after a stellar high school career at Notre Dame High in the San Fernando Valley, transferred from Michigan. And other recruits, such as Mater Dei quarterback Matt Leinart, who had wavered on their commitments to Troy after Hackett was fired, re-upped with the school.

Carroll also hired a knowledgeable and respected staff that included offensive coordinator Norm Chow. And through it all, no one ever questioned the head coach's ability as an Xs and Os man. "The longer I was around him, the more I respected his coaching ability," Donaldson said. Carroll's hiring was "like a layup," Gross said.

Still the Trojans won only two of their first seven games in Carroll's debut in 2001, a bottom line that, if anything, looked even worse than the Hackett era. Then senior cornerback Kris

Prize recruit Shaun Cody helped usher in the Pete Carroll era.

Joe Robbins

Richard returned an interception 58 yards for a touchdown late in the fourth quarter to beat Arizona in Tucson. And since then USC has been nearly unstoppable, putting together a three-plus season run never seen before, not even in Troy's heyday of the 1970s.

The numbers are staggering. Including that win over the Wildcats, the Trojans won forty of forty-four games through the end of the 2004 season. They outscored their opponents 1,640–719 in that span (an average score of 37–16). Their thirty-six victories from 2002 to 2004 were the most they ever amassed in a three-year stretch in their history. Their twenty-one consecutive wins at the Coliseum from 2001 to 2004 set a school record. Their thirteen victories in 2004 set another all-time mark.

In 2002 USC quarterback Carson Palmer won the Heisman Trophy. Two years later Leinart won it. The 2004 squad featured six first-team All-Americans, the most ever at Troy. All this on the heels of a 5–7 season in 2000, the last year before Carroll arrived. That's a long way in a short time. "This program is flying," Carroll said after beating the Sooners.

Before the Trojans could fly again, though, they had to learn to get off the ground. After USC beat San Jose State 21–10 in Carroll's first game in 2001, the Trojans dropped four winnable games in a row: 10–6 to number-twelve Kansas State, 24–22 at number-seven Oregon on a field goal with 12 seconds left, 21–16 to Stanford, and 27–24 at number-eleven Washington on a field goal as time ran out. By season's end Troy's 6–6 record included five losses of 5 points or fewer.

It was more of the same early in 2002. USC began the season ranked eighteenth in the nation, but stood only 3–2 after

The Streak

After dropping a 34–31 decision in three overtimes at California in the fourth game of 2003, USC did not lose another game that season or the next. Here's how the Trojans forged their twenty-two-game winning streak (entering 2005):

2003

October 4	W	37	at Arizona State	17
October 11	W	44	Stanford	21
October 18	W	45	at Notre Dame	14
October 25	W	43	at Washington	23
November 1	W	43	Washington State	16
November 15	W	45	at Arizona	0
November 22	W	47	UCLA	22
December 6	W	52	Oregon State	28
January 1	W	28	Michigan (Rose Bowl)	14

2004

August 28	W	24	Virginia Tech (Landover, MD)	13
September 11	W	49	Colorado State	0
September 18	W	42	at BYU	10
September 25	W	31	at Stanford	28
October 9	W	23	California	17
October 16	W	45	Arizona State	7
October 23	W	38	Washington	0
October 30	W	42	at Washington State	12
November 6	W	28	at Oregon State	20
November 13	W	49	Arizona	9
November 27	W	41	Notre Dame	10
December 4	W	29	at UCLA	24
January 4	W	55	Oklahoma (Orange Bowl)	19

The 2004 squad was the first to win thirteen games in a season. *Joe Robbins*

dropping a pair of difficult decisions at number-twenty-five Kansas State (27–20) and at number-seventeen Washington State (30–27 in overtime). But in game six the Trojans overcame a 21–3 first-half deficit at home to California and stormed back to win 30–28.

From then on Palmer and Troy's offense were nearly unstoppable against a gauntlet of formidable opponents. USC put up 41 points against number-twenty-two Washington; 44 at number-fourteen Oregon; 49 at Stanford; 34 against Arizona State; 52 at number-twenty-five UCLA; and 44 against number-seven Notre Dame, a game in which Troy piled up an Irish opponents' record 625 total yards. At 10–2, the fifth-ranked Trojans earned a Bowl Championship Series berth for the first time, and they pummeled number-three Iowa 38–17. USC was clearly back on the national stage. The Trojans would move front and center in 2003.

Though hopes for an undefeated season were dashed with a 34–31 triple-overtime loss at California in the fourth game, Carroll's team responded with arguably the most critical victory of his tenure the following week, rallying for a 37–17 victory at Arizona State behind an injured Leinart.

Despite the loss to the Bears, the Trojans still were a top-ten team and, as it turned out, still in the national title hunt heading into their game against the Sun Devils. But the game was tied at 10–10 at halftime, and Leinart was in the locker room nursing an injured knee and a twisted ankle that kept him out the second quarter.

Working behind a veteran offensive line and with capable receivers such as senior Keary Colbert and sophomore sensation Mike Williams, Leinart had been solid, though not yet spectacular as Palmer's successor, passing for 924 yards and 8 touchdowns in the first four games. He'd also been intercepted 6 times. But with backup Matt Cassel warming up on the sidelines, Leinart hobbled back onto the field in the third quarter and proved he was ready to lead this team.

Arizona State scored early in the third quarter to take a 17–10 lead, but the Trojans countered with a touchdown march capped by LenDale White's 25-yard scoring run. Then Leinart tossed a 33-yard touchdown pass to fullback Brandon Hancock on fourth-and-1 to give USC the lead.

Matt Leinart quarterbacked USC's back-to-back national championships in 2003 and 2004. Joe Robbins

After that the Trojans never looked back—not that day and not in any game since. It was the first of USC's nation-leading, twenty-two-game winning streak and the second longest in school history, behind the twenty-five in a row won by the 1931–33 squads.

Win number eight in the string came against Michigan in the Rose Bowl on January 1, 2004. The Trojans' convincing 28–14 victory over the Wolverines gave USC the Associated Press's half of the national championship.

Upset that the top-ranked team in the nation was snubbed for the BCS title game in favor of number-two Oklahoma and number-three LSU, Carroll and his team handled the situation with class and dignity—and then came back with a vengeance in 2004.

Leinart, working with a whole new set of receivers and a revamped offensive line that had lost several seniors from the year before, showed leadership and poise while guiding Troy past every challenge.

Oddly the last hurdle was perhaps the easiest. With a month to prepare for the Orange Bowl, Carroll's defensive schemes and Chow's offensive plan were too much for Oklahoma. (It turned out to be Chow's last game before taking a similar job in the NFL.) The Sooners marched more than 90 yards to a touchdown the first time they had the ball, but it was all USC after that.

Tight end Dominique Byrd's highlight-reel, one-handed, 33-yard touchdown catch soon tied the score, and then the Trojans converted four Oklahoma turnovers into 24 points before intermission. It was 38–10 at halftime, and it was just a matter of time before the postgame podium was set up to honor the Trojans as back-to-back national champs. "Something really special is happening here, and we're just loving being a part of it," Carroll said.

It sure looked as if the Trojans were having fun all night. Palmer, the former Heisman Trophy–winning quarterback, was on the sidelines during the game. Two years earlier he had closed his USC career by leading Troy past Iowa 38–17 on the same field. He knew then that something special was happening at USC. "I just wish I could be around for it," he said wistfully at the time.

Palmer graduated to the NFL, where the Cincinnati Bengals selected him with the first pick in the 2003 draft and helped ease any longing for his college days with a multimillion-dollar contract. Meanwhile Carroll reloaded with Leinart at quarterback the following season. Faced with the prospect of potentially losing Leinart to the pros after his junior season in 2004 (Leinart eventually decided to return for his senior year in 2005), the coach was not fazed on the night of the Orange Bowl.

"This program is bigger than just one guy," he said. "We can't wait to see who does something special next."